P9-CLU-909

TELEVISION:
the medium and
its manners

TELEVISION:
the medium and
its manners

Peter Conrad

Routledge & Kegan Paul
Boston, London and Henley

First published in 1982
by Routledge & Kegan Paul Ltd
9 Park Street, Boston, Mass. 02108, USA,
39 Store Street, London WC1E 7DD and
Broadway House, Newtown Road,
Henley-on-Thames, Oxon RG9 1EN
Set in 11 on 13pt Sabon by
Rowland Phototypesetting Ltd, Bury St Edmunds, Suffolk
and printed in the USA
© Peter Conrad, 1982
No part of this book may be reproduced in
any form without permission from the
publisher, except for the quotation of brief
passages in criticism

ISBN 0-7100-9040-4
ISBN 0-7100-9041-2 (pbk)

V. S.W.
Gift of publisher
May 2, 1984

Visual Studies Workshop
Research Center
Rochester, N.Y.

Contents

1
Furniture

In the Oxford college to which I belong, a television set has been supplied for the delectation of the brain-weary dons. It's hidden away in a musty chamber, bottling up the fug of defunct cigars, called the smoking room. In a corner of that room, it stands masquerading as a Gothic cocktail cabinet, concealed behind panels of fretted wood which have to be opened out like an altar diptych to disclose the screen. People sometimes scuttle across the quad after dark to watch it, conscious (in their furtiveness) that in doing so they're neglecting their pedagogic chores, and the set they watch is as ashamed as they are. Hence its elaborate decorative lie about itself, its nervous attempt to disappear into the seedy antiquity of the room. When you open the doors of that cumbrous box you expect to find cut-glass decanters collared with silver chains identifying the type of toxic spirit they contain. Instead you happen upon a gaping field of grey plastic which is the empty screen.

Why is the television set our dirty domestic secret? Why are we so apologetic about owning one? The dons of Oxford are not alone in their decorative disavowal of the medium. Often in highbrow households the set will be found snugly lodged in a wall of bookshelves, as if proximity could make an ersatz literary object of it. The vulgarly rich have devised more expensive ways to hide it, and the video magazines illustrate ideal living rooms in which the set plays at being something other than itself, either lurking under a tailored cloth impersonating an end table or cowering inside cabinets with doors which can be pulled down like portcullises to occlude the screen. The most ingenious and costly disappearances are contrived by the New York designer Anthony Lombardo, who banishes the set behind magnesium mirrors in a wall of carved panelling, with cane-covered vents above the mantel for the audio outlets. The skulking telly is enticed out of hiding by activating a remote control, and its image glimmers in the depths of the suddenly transparent looking-glass. Sets installed by Lombardo are the perfection of discreet self-effacement, for they can be viewed without being seen. He has even absconded a set behind tambour doors in the belly of a white baby grand piano.

In contrast with this swanky snubbing of television, in suburban houses the set is encouraged to perform as furniture, propped on a trolley which can be perambulated into hiding but which, while in the room, serves up the programmes as delicacies: the trolleys recall those which fancy restaurants trundle about, loaded with their display of sweets. Perhaps a vase of flowers is lodged atop the set, to acclimatise it; I have also seen a set hooked and suspended from the ceiling like a potted plant. If company arrives when you're watching, the set will probably be left playing, with the volume muffled. This will justify it as a social amenity, a supplier, like piped music in public places, of automatic conviviality, both an encouragement to and (during awkward silences) a relief from conversation. Always the set has to be supplied with an alibi, an excuse for its presence in and appropriation of the room. In one household I know, a place of no social pretension, an atlas is left casually lying on the table next to the set. 'Why?' I once asked. 'So we can look up where all those wars are happening that we see on television,' I was told. Thus the set legitimises itself as an educational facility, plugging you into the world outside the house. The shiftiest of all television-owners are those who smuggle their sets into their bedrooms. Out in the living room it at least pretends to be of social use. Propped at the bottom of your bed, it stands exposed as the most consolingly solitary of vices. Andy Warhol has even likened masturbation to watching a made-for-TV movie, as opposed to the self-forgetful enchantments of the big screen and the dark auditorium: you resign yourself sadly to an unsatisfying second best. In the living room, the set is a substitute for conversation; in here by the bed, it's a substitute for – and an approximation to – sleep, its inane, inconstant flickering turning the room into the delusory prison of Plato's cave-dweller.

Our shame about television twists into superstitious fear. There's a code of manners for television-viewing, with rules to save us from the consequences of our dangerous and unseemly habit. Leave a light on in the room to protect your eyes from damage by the tube; unplug the set at night, or else it's liable to sizzle, explode and incinerate the house in which it's such an unwelcome tenant. The British *Television Annual* in the early 1950s contained worried articles on the domestic havoc the new invention was likely to cause. The set's invasion of the house was a cue for disputes over where to locate it. The *Annual* recommended compromises and placation: 'the main need is to put the set where viewing will be the most comfortable, avoiding the possibility of half the family being shielded from the fire while the other half is roasted on top of it!' This particular contingency was soon disposed of, once television displaced the hearth. Owners were warned to beware of their fickle, combustible possession, told to earth it and enjoined to 'Never Go Beyond the Named Controls – . . . *do not* poke about inside the television receiver.'

Intruding into the home, the television set declared war on

it, announcing that our living space was no longer to be a familial sanctuary, in which things are venerated because they're outdated and have memories attaching to them, but an insulated, efficient, impersonal contraption. Le Corbusier despised the ancestral home as a squalid mud hut. Modern man was to be resettled in a habitable machine, in the company of his technological appliances. The *Television Annual* sentimentally arrests this necessary change, showing television aerials sprouting from the thatched roofs of Suffolk cottages: the old way of life, it hoped, could be wired up to the technological sensorium without disruption. The 1952 *Annual* included a section on 'The Announcers Off Duty' which, in following the performers home, was covertly domesticating and pastoralising the inimical gadgetry of television. One announcer describes his local country pub, another is pictured serving nursery tea 'in the quiet house hidden away below the Sussex Downs', a third declares, 'I like home best.' All of them are solemnly repudiating their profession, adhering to the rural and domestic retirement which television was abolishing.

The early sets were likewise self-denying or self-confounding in design, veneering or inlaying themselves with grained walnut, limed oak, Indian laurel or mahogany, pretending to be ornament not electronic equipment. This recalls the Victorian embarrassment with utility, the decorative euphemism which sheathed chairs in antimacassars, pudically curtained table legs, and named railway engines after chivalric warriors; but there's more to it than that. Our bad conscience about having surrendered our living rooms to the television set hints at our resentment of the technology to which (according to Marshall McLuhan) we ought to be so grateful. McLuhan delighted in technology as a divine comedy. Human beings, he believed, had been ushered into an earthly paradise by their appliances, which freed them from Adam's curse of physical toil, made life Edenically easy and blissful once more, and messianically extended their feeble, fallen bodily capacities. The truth is subtler and more disgruntled than this mystical Catholic second coming. Our attitude to our appliances is complicated by frustration at our dependence on them and their arcane independence of us. At any time they may spurn us, as those dire portents in the *Television Annual* imply. Much as we try to love them, we know we can't trust them. They're aliens which have requisitioned our houses, and we'd all like to fight back by damaging them – if only we didn't own them. Television sets aren't the only objects of this equivocal emotion. Think of the curious relation Americans have with their cars. They wash and polish and carpet them and bring them indoors like pet animals by constructing carports to shelter them. In New Jersey in September 1980 a couple was taken into custody while finalising a McLuhanesque transaction in a used-car lot: they'd been caught trading in their 14-month-old child in return for a 3-year-old sports car, admitting in doing so that they'd sooner have possessions than offspring. But Americans are also elated by the reckless destruction of those expensive, demanding and unreliable machines, in demolition derbies, freeway pile-ups and rusting cemeteries of junked cars. We're afraid of the frauds committed by salesmen and of the obsolescence to which the object – whether it's a car or a television set – is soon to be condemned, because the manufacturers have by malign determination made it imperfect and temporary. This is why the proverbial association of Nixon with a used car was so damning. He was both the mendacious car salesman and the dubious vehicle itself, unable to keep its promises to us. The development of television was hindered by this suspicion of technology. People were wary of buying sets because the transmission standard was constantly altering, leaving them with useless receivers. When the British service began in 1936, the government could only guarantee the scanning standard until the end of 1938; repeated assurances that no more changes were anticipated had to be issued during the 1950s, to allay this fear.

For us, the definition of an exhilaratingly gratuitous act – a deed which recklessly expends pure and unmotivated will – is the destruction of a television set. The angry adolescent kicks and shatters a television screen, to the maid's horror, in Bertolucci's *La Luna*, and at the end of *Zabriskie Point* Antonioni stages an apocalyptic detonation of consumer durables: television sets splinter, refrigerators explode, houses erupt, in a cleansing, vengeful fury. At the Cow Palace in San Francisco on 4 July 1975 a 'media burn' neatly combined the combustibility of the television set with the obsolescence of the automobile: a customised car hurtled through a pyramid of burning television sets, while a crowd cheered deliriously. As these acts of reprisal suggest, we love to hate our appliances. For though they have beguiled us with their offer of relief, they have also conspired to enslave us. Television doesn't divert us when we choose but by implanting habits weakens our choice and makes us its patient, lobotomised 'viewers'. Hence its alliance, which later chapters on ads and game shows will explore, with the ideology of consumerism, for just as television recruits and conscripts us as its viewers, so the market defines us as consumers, the docile maws into which it can pump goods we don't need but which it convinces us we can't do without. The very word appliance is tainted with medical shame. It's used as well of surgical aids, artificial limbs, and plastic choppers: these too are what McLuhan would call 'extensions of man'. Our gadgets are our prostheses. We have our ways of humbling them, however. We can be as promiscuous as they are – trading them in before they wear out, divorcing them before they have the chance to betray us; or hiding them in the decor of the houses they want to dominate. More recent technological gimmickry has allowed us to enslave them, rather than numbly acquiescing in their dictatorship. Armed with a dismissive remote control baton you can make the set dizzy, ordering it – in America at least, where there are so many stations – to respond to your own impatience by flicking through its entire repertoire of channels in a few seconds. Video recorders as well are a contradiction of the set they supplement. Not only do they free us from the schedule the set imposes on us, they equip the forgetful form of television, addicted to the transitory present, with a memory.

McLuhan's account of television in *Understanding Media* (1964) suited the astrological optimism of its decade. The book is a religious tract, quoting a directive from the Vatican to justify its immersion in the media and pining for a condition of 'wholeness' and 'empathy' (contrived by the new electric technology) which resembles other Catholic fantasies, whether historical, like G. K. Chesterton's pious version of the Middle Ages, or metaphysical, like Teilhard de Chardin's nöosphere. McLuhan houses the television set in a tabernacle, and its flicker signals an electronic annunciation. He describes the new 'depth awareness' of the decade, which has been cultivated by the media, as a state of religious afflatus: 'there is a deep faith to be found in this new attitude – a faith that concerns the ultimate harmony of all being.' McLuhan wants to understand media in order to convert them to this faith, to 'bring them into orderly service'. But to me the evidence suggests that the media aren't spiritual ministers and comforters to us: it's we, on the contrary, who serve them. McLuhan sees the long reign of literacy as a privation, a regime of asceticism which the sensory bombardment of the new media has triumphantly ended. Like a second coming, television retribalises a society which typography fragmented and secularised, and beatifies its viewers. McLuhan's book castigates books. Watching young children cowering over books held a few inches from their faces, he reflects that they are 'striving to carry over to the printed page the all-involving sensory mandate of the TV image'. For McLuhan, the children aren't to be blamed for their stumbling illiteracy. It's the books which are at fault, unable to deliver the engulfing experience for which we long. Television requires this participation in depth, relying as it does on the viewer to 'complete what is only hinted at in the mosaic mesh of dots'. It's therefore a remedy for our spiritual impoverishment. But McLuhan is wrong about this ecstatic involvement. Television sentences us instead to passivity and bored indifference. We can wander off at will because the programmes create their own intervals to appease our inattention; we can slither absently from channel to channel. We are far from acknowledging that debt of religious gratitude which McLuhan believed we owe to our appliances.

In its early years television diplomatically sensed our resentment and went out of its way to pacify us, apologising for its intrusion into our houses, our habits and our minds. Its performers comported themselves as if they were our perhaps unwelcome guests. By choosing to watch them, we were issuing a social invitation to them. At the end of his show Red Skelton used to thank his audiences for having invited him into their living rooms. But the medium didn't remain deferential for long. Television, at first the obsequious intruder, soon became convinced that it had more right to occupy our houses than we, its messy unelectronic legatees, did. The comedian Ernie Kovacs therefore slyly twisted askew Skelton's courtesy by demanding that the house makes itself worthy of the set: his line was 'Thank you for inviting me into your house – but couldn't you have cleaned it up a bit?'

Despite Kovacs's joke, the scruples of polite social conduct are still held to govern the behaviour of television people. Life inside the box must match the life in the room where the box is situated. Thus through the course of the television day, the cameras, like the set itself, move from room to room in the viewer's house. The soap operas and the ads which interrupt them take place in the kitchen because that's where they expect to be watched, by wives spending the morning and the dreary afternoon at their indentured labour of scrubbing and scouring. By evening the set has shifted to the living room where the reassembled family groups around it. The patriarch of the American evening news, Walter Cronkite, was trusted because, as was regularly said of him, he was the kind of man you'd happily invite into your living room. By 11.30 p.m. the set has advanced to the bedroom, and so have the programmes. A writer for *The Tonight Show* comments that 'Johnny Carson comes right into the bedroom', which explains public toleration of his raunchiness. He's the midnight, satyr-like antithesis of Cronkite: in place of the tribal elder solemnising contemporary events we have the impudent Carson who, in the privacy of the bedroom, can gossip scabrously in his monologues about those same public figures who earlier in the evening were treated with such gravity by Cronkite. Carson knows that the tone of his show is determined by the room in which it's supposedly watched, and refers to *The Tonight Show* as 'NBC's alternative to foreplay'. Enterprising motels in New York and California have progressed even further than Carson in equating what happens on the screen with what transpires in the room housing the set. Here the television is enlisted to encourage and accompany the couplings of those who rent the room: the sets are supplied with pornographic videocassettes, so you can make love in voyeuristic competition with limbre professionals.

Television begins by miming our passage through the day and through the house, but ends by directing it. The box is no longer our guest, conscious (as in Red Skelton's goodbye) of being on probation. Now it imposes its schedules on us, and defines our reality according to its own convenience. During the day the ads scale a crescendo of consumerism. In the morning and afternoon they concentrate on polishes, detergents, toilet tissue, the articles within the housewife's domain; in the evening these domestic trifles are supplanted by cars, airlines, commercial banks, all the prerogatives of the money-making male. Late at night, when we're watching in bed, television advertises beds which – if we bought one of them – would relieve us from the need to watch late-night television. *The Tonight Show* is regularly interrupted by an ad for a posturepedic, adjustable bed, which derides the desperate use of television as an alternative to sleep. A wife with an aching back wakes her husband. 'Another night of watching television,' he groans, vowing to buy one of those beds he's seen advertised on television, which can be manipulated to soothe the insomniac. He grins out of the screen and admonishes we morose nocturnal viewers: 'if you had a posturepedic bed, you'd be asleep by now,' by which he means that we wouldn't be condemned to a night-long television vigil. This is one of consumerism's smuggest put-downs of the medium with which it has such a special relationship. Television's purpose is to sell us things. If we bought them, we wouldn't need to watch television.

The schedules don't merely follow the course of the week but impose their own shape on it. Since Monday is the resumption of the working week, on British television it's the day for programmes documenting the intractable realities of the world: *Panorama, World in Action.* Tuesday, Wednesday and Thursday are days of routine and repetition, on television as off, and the schedules are therefore occupied with serials, which derive a virtue from predictability. On Friday and Saturday there are late-night movies, and the preferred genres are horror and crime, because this has been decreed by the networks as a time for harmlessly vicious or larcenous fantasy, for holiday emotion. The idleness of our weekends is occupied by a paradoxical celebration of action, in which other people exert themselves on our behalf: sports on Saturday, westerns on Sunday afternoon. At the weekend, the news is abbreviated and at irregular hours, as if nothing would have the temerity to happen during this period of remission. Twice recently the newsmen have been disconcerted because things did happen on days they'd declared off-limits. The murder of Mountbatten occurred on that most otiose of dates, an August Bank Holiday Monday in 1979; and the fiery end to the Iranian Embassy siege in London in May 1980 also came on a Bank Holiday.

Permitting television to fill up our lives, we've suffered it to regulate them. Granting it entry into our houses as furniture, we've allowed it to take over those houses. In the 1950s a fan of the CBS *Today Show* demolished a wall between his breakfast area and his living room so he could watch the programme before leaving for work. Other devotees, in those days before a household could afford a set for each room, rigged up arrangements of mirrors so they could see round corners. To the American networks, the loyalty of the viewers was attested by their willingness to modify or even knock down their houses in order to accommodate the set. The British were more circumspect, but still preoccupied with reorganising their houses as receivers. Americans did so by a flair for destruction, like that fan of *The Today Show*; the British did so not by hollowing out their houses but by insulating them from the nuisance of the interfering world outside. The *Television Annual* compiles a neurasthenic digest of the enemies of the picture – motor traffic, hair driers, factory equipment; gasometers or pylons cause fluttery ghosts; viewers near hospitals will be tormented by waves from systems for diathermy treatment. 'The only remedy', the *Annual* starchily counsels, 'is suppression at the source, and by reporting such cases to the local post office' (where complaint forms were provided) 'this may in time be achieved'. During the corporate battle between CBS and RCA over the colour television system, the set was temporarily cast as a cranky, marauding engine, liable to erupt in the sedate living room it had invaded: a manufacturer of black and white sets sought to protect its own interests by alarming the public with a mock-up of a gigantic colour wheel, spinning at dangerous speeds, which would be one of the colour set's components, and asking the federal commissioners to imagine the devastation the wheel would cause if it whirred out of control.

Television is a box ensconced in the rooms we inhabit, and this fact governs and limits the kind of reality we see inside that box. Television people are tenants or perhaps internees of the box. The medium's aim is to contrive an equation between what happens in the box and what happens in front of it. In looking at the screen, we're meant to see our own lives reflected. Though it's a miniaturisation of ourselves we gaze at, we're persuaded to accept it as the truth. An ad for Channel 7 *Eyewitness News*, published in the New York *Village Voice* in February 1980, makes this point elegantly, converting the set into an ornate portrait frame to hang on our wall and also into a looking-glass through which we travel when we look into it. Under a headline promising that 'our heart is where your home is', the news team is seen lined up, smiling cheesily, inside a gilt frame. There's an initial disparity between the contents of the image and the room in which the image is located. The frame stands on a doily-covered table, flanked by a coiling candlestick and a single rose in a vase; behind it is a blurry flocked wallpaper. But the frame encloses technological modernity. Looking into it, we see what's behind the camera: the electronic innards of the set. The reporters, though as benign and friendly as a Victorian family ranked in tiers for a photograph, are squatting on metal chairs or perched on ladders, environed by the paraphernalia of their trade – cameras, cables, booms, a hoisted microphone. Though inmates of the box, they belong among our domestic furniture. Though marooned down the cathode tube in their own unreality, they profess not only to describe our reality but to share it. The ad goes on to call them 'the home team', good reporters who are good neighbours and who deserve to be billeted in our living rooms: 'everyone on the team shares a great concern for our community. Not only on the job but on their own. Which means that you're just as likely to see them around town as on the air.' Guaranteeing that the journalists walk the streets like the rest of us, the ad's copy does seem to grant its personnel a life outside the immurement of their medium, but the photograph argues differently. Collaring twenty-one people and their equipment inside a picture-frame which looks like a filigree television set and planting them on a living room table, the ad is proposing a direct transmission from one box to another which is a replica of it – from the television studio via the set to the house which duplicates the studio, because there the family is arrayed to smile welcomingly at a corps of news reporters who are themselves a jocund, neighbourly family. The signal beamed between boxes misses that outer air – the world beyond the confines of studio, set and living room – which is its presumed subject. This is television's ambition: to make life as much as possible like television; to operate within a charmed and closed circuit of self-reference.

Another ad brags of this ambivalent boon. One of television's favours to us is to make everything as easy as watching television. Thus when the San Francisco Opera production of Ponchielli's *La Gioconda* was relayed, one digestible act to an evening, between April 14 and 17 in 1980, Channel 13 in New York engaged a copy-writer whose cunning and invidious pitch was to contrast the fearful exposure and rare virtuosity of the opera's performers with the factitious domestic comfort of the viewers. The opera, we're told, is terrifyingly difficult and expensive to produce, and makes outrageous demands on its singers; but all we have to do is sit down, settle back, and watch. The experience of the opera on television is commended to us not as an acceptable substitute for the experience we'd have had in the theatre but as the opposite of it, and an improvement on it. You don't have to make the effort to go out ('Pull up an easy chair,' the copy invites). Nor do you have to spend money (you get, the ad winsomely insists, 'five nights of opera for a song'). *La Gioconda* with its festive mobs, its nautical battles, its inflated sentiments, altitudinous voices and uproarious noise, has been squeezed into the box and deposited in our houses as a small and undemanding piecemeal package, and with superb effrontery television doesn't apologise for its denaturing of the object but contends that the offending article – hitherto undemocratically arduous, requiring from us an effort of attention and the disbursement of money – has been bettered in the process. Like the ad for *Eyewitness News*, which rebuilds the studio in our living room, that for *La Gioconda* doesn't show the gaudy trinketry of the opera house or the spectacular affray on stage but flatteringly represents the room in which the performance will be watched, for that room, the box's auditorium, is now the measure of the event it temporarily contains. Under the banner 'See *La Gioconda* from the best seats in the house' there's an inset sketch of two unoccupied arm-chairs drawn up against a wall, separated by a table on which stand a lamp, a vase, and a family photograph. With odd realistic exactness, the lamp is even supplied with a cord which trails to a wall-plug under the table – television's reminder, perhaps, that the source of its illusion is electricity, not (as in the opera) straining human vocal cords or the orchestral combinations of wood, metal and fibre; that the dream can be plugged in and switched on at will. Television never neutrally allows an event to pass through it. In transit, a change occurs, and the medium, aware of its power, feels free to prefer its diminished and domesticated version of an event like *La Gioconda* to the outsize, unruly original.

Television's astutest performers are those who recognise that they're captives of the box and, instead of chafing against it, rejoice in their imprisonment. They don't pine for a less claustrophobic stage or for rapport with an audience. They're satisfied with the camera for company, and with the addition after the event of taped applause. The television comedian gets his laughs from the gadgetry. The camera, not those who are on the other side of it, is his court of appeal. In 1954 Milton

Berle designed the Berlite, for shows without a studio audience. Lights blink on when laughter or applause are required, these are mixed in by the audio engineers, and 'the sound comes through the camera', as if the camera itself were chortling. The alienatory wit of the medium was a constant subject in the show George Burns and Gracie Allen shared in the 1950s. Burns knew they were on television, Gracie didn't. Once on the show he asked her what she thought of television. She replied that she loved it: 'I hardly ever watch radio any more.' Gracie superstitiously ignored the camera's presence. In their first season, when the show was transmitted live, she caught sight of the light on the camera which warned her that it was watching and recording her. It so unnerved her that she never looked that way again. Burns, by contrast, owed his persona of comic superiority to his understanding and exploitation of the medium. Not only did he address the camera, in those smirking monologues which opened and closed the show, he also watched the intervening action on television. In his den he had a television screen which, when he fiddled with its knobs, showed him what was happening elsewhere in the house. He could use the medium against Gracie, to spy on her and catch her out, and he also tersely educated her in the manners appropriate to the new form, telling her at the end of each show to say good night – not so much to the studio audience as to the camera. Burns's snide partnership with the camera, like Berle's solicitation of a mechanical laughter from it, devised a technique for the medium which by now has become an automatic reflex: the game show hosts wink or leer at the camera when they succeed in embarrassing their victims; Johnny Carson imparts to the camera reserved for his solitary use his grimaces of astonishment at the follies of his guests, even ostentatiously stifling a yawn when on a recent show Tony Randall began to deliver a lecturette on etymology.

In the movies, you have to conquer the camera obliquely, without ever betraying your interest in it. The great movie stars tease and frustrate the camera by affecting to ignore it. Movie faces must be impervious: Garbo's cold, marbled mask; Chaplin's absence of expression; Marilyn Monroe with her defensive, myopic look, half way between bemusement and wry detachment, as if (as in *How to Marry a Millionaire*) she was hiding behind a misty pair of spectacles to ward off the camera's passes. These people all defy the camera to trespass on their mystery. One of them, the mumbling Brando, defies the microphone as well. They seduce us and the camera because they can never be completely known or understood. But television's rule is the opposite: you must besiege the camera with your attentions, win it over by grimacing at it like Lucille Ball or gravely pacifying it like Cronkite, transforming your reactions into facial tics for it as Carson does. Being on television is about being on television. If you forget the medium and its unreality, you fail.

Gracie Allen was startled and dismayed when she noticed the camera scrutinising her. We as viewers are likewise not just the spectators of the box: it watches us in its turn. The viewer's destiny is to be enrolled by that obnoxious box, which wants to make us accountable to it. American public broadcasting stations during their fund-raising sprees appeal to the viewer to 'become a member of public television' by sending in a donation. It's not enough to watch television: you have to join it. In Britain, where you have to pay a licence fee to legitimise your ownership of the set, the BBC has detector vans touring the suburbs, checking on those who haven't paid their dues. The unlicensed viewer is a lawbreaker, and the severest penalty is confiscation of the renegade set: the ads warn that, if found out, you may have to sell your set to pay the fine. America too has its electronic definition of good citizenship. Using demographic data from the government census, the Nielsen Company selects 1,200 homes and by tabulating their viewing habits decides on a national set of ratings to which the networks defer. The company calls its selection of households a 'sample universe' – a box-sized microcosm of America, an imaginary statistical village deputising for a continent. The moment we switch on our sets, we're offering up information about ourselves, agreeing to be studied as a statistic. Television is furniture which talks back. While we're trustfully ogling it, it's monitoring us.

2
Technology

Television is an optical illusion to which technology gives credence. It depends, like magic, on the eye's willingness to be deceived, to sort the blitz of dots with which the tube bombards us into a picture. Television exists between the chimerae of magic and the miracles which science accomplishes mechanically. It elucidates technical advances by translating them back into magic stunts. When in 1955 the British independent network began broadcasting, viewers had to switch between channels of varying signal-strength. Pye developed a means of automatic picture control which kept the tonality steady despite changes in the signal, but their advertisements explained this new circuitry as carnival magic not electronics: the automatic control was represented by a giant's fist which gripped the waist of a playfully struggling girl. Those fickle, flickery signals are feminine; the new circuit which restrains them is the long arm of male stability and reassurance. The box was from the first an object of nervous wonder, since it harbours a technical voodoo. The early ads always show people dressed up in their finery to watch it, with expressions of amazement on their faces. A miracle has been deposited in their living rooms, and they cluster round it with a devout concentration which alleviates their uneasiness. When asked how we're going to spend the evening, we still tend to say 'watching television' without specifying which programmes we intend to watch: it's the box we're watching, regardless of what's on it; it's the medium we marvel at, not its ephemeral messages.

The first sets were displayed at the World's Fair of 1939 in New York, in a pavilion shaped like a radio tube, and the start of public broadcasting in New York coincided with the opening of the fair. The occasion was significant. The World's Fair was an emporium of technological modernity and a prevision of the future. Those antique sets reveal, as the fair did, science in competition with the recondite projections of science fiction, for they belong dually to technology and to magic: their cumbrous mechanical bulk marks them as intricate systems of gadgetry, but they're also a magician's devious kit, concealing tricks of illusion. The shape of these sets was determined by technical necessity, but these technical compromises only confirmed the suggestion of wizardry. For instance, in some of the early sets – among them the 1937 Baird T-5 – you didn't look at the image directly. The cathode tubes in these models were almost three feet long, and mounted upright. The image was passed to a mirror poised at an angle on the top of the cabinet, its surface silvered to prevent doubling. The mirror was practical: the picture on the end of the cathode-ray tube was inverted, and had to be reversed before it could be deciphered. But it looked magical. The set became an arcane periscope, guarding its mystery inside that tall and bulky cabinet, permitting us only to spy on it indirectly, because we have the mirror to mediate for us.

There was another potentially absurd disparity in those early sets between the size and weight of the wooden casing and their tiny picture-screens. The reason was technical. The cabinet had to house its own mains transformer, dispensed with after the war when sets derived their high-voltage supply from the scanning circuit which delineated the picture. Yet this contradiction also served to emphasise the wonder of the process whereby that lumbering box laboured to bring forth an image as small (in 1938 models) as five inches. When this screen was inflated it looked even more of a technological freak. Some 1948 sets had convex bubbles of perspex fixed in front of the picture and mounted on a frame. These were looking-glasses conducting us into the recess of unreality behind the screen, and a science-fiction laboratory's blow-up of the human eye – for the technology of television is a replica of the eye's management of the signals it receives. After the war, ray tubes acquired rectangular faces and an increased scanning angle, so the screens became larger while the cabinets shrank, rectifying the earlier disproportion. But still owners liked to subject the image to transformations of their own, which gave them the sensation of summoning it up like technological abracadabra in their living rooms. Philips developed a projection receiver, which enlarged the image to four feet by five feet by reflecting it from a concave mirror through a correcting plate; you could also attach a filter to the screen, shielding it from light in the room.

The self-confident medium creates around it places which are representations of its own inner workings and specimens of the future it envisages for us. Its studios are television sets expanded. Hence the aptness of its location in that tube-shaped pavilion at the World's Fair; and the hint of this pavilion was taken up by the studio NBC designed in the 1950s for its early morning programme, *The Today Show*. The show was intended to awake America, both literally and symbolically – to jolly its viewers through breakfast and equip them for the day ahead with news headlines, weather reports, time checks and traffic warnings, but also to adjust them to membership of a world whose remotest corners now overlapped, by the grace of technology, inside their television sets. The executive who devised the show, Sylvester Weaver, wanted its decor to actualise the millennial future in which television belonged.

The studio's furnishings were to demonstrate the televisual simultaneity of all times and places – clocks for each of the world's time zones, samplings of regional newspapers to be scanned and synopsised by the cameras, rattling wire reports and jangling telephones. The compere was less a host than a presiding and co-ordinating intelligence, for whom Weaver invented the allegorical title 'The Communicator'. The network's publicity referred to *The Today Show*'s headquarters as a 'World Communications Center' and 'The Nerve Center of the Planet', a brain despatching electronic ganglia to the extremities of a world conceived as a single sprawling but manipulable body. Weaver dreamed of a studio designed to be as modern as the interior of a television set, glass-walled to admit the lucid and rational sun, with the newsroom on the floor but balconies jutting from the walls high above it. The news when transmitted was meant to take to the air: on the ledges acolytes could perch, thrilling to the vibrations of a message-laden ether.

As its base, the programme was assigned a store front on West 49th Street in New York, in Radio City. This had been previously used for exhibiting RCA's newest television sets. Now it became a distended and transparent television set. People gathered on the street to stare through the picture window into the future and watch its adepts at their unsleeping work. Aimed outwards from the studio into the street, the cameras in their turn saw in the crowd of onlookers a world which was battling to squeeze itself into the television screen, clamouring to have its reality validated by electronic reproduction. The sidewalk on 49th Street became a forum convened by television, the shared public space of citizenship. Out-of-towners would turn up to jostle for a place near the glass so they could wave mute greetings to their relatives back home during the show; protestors held placards above the heads of the crowd. What the camera saw was not a global village but a continent fitting neatly inside the box, like the 'sample universe' of the Nielsen sociologists. The informal political status of this gathering was confirmed one morning when President Truman, out for a walk, turned up among the peeping-toms in the street: we're now all enrolled as subjects of the television screen, and because these people were television-watchers and volunteer television-performers, they served as a constituency for Truman. As well as conferring citizenship, television was bestowing celebrity on those watchers on the other side of the window. For they were all ambitious to journey through that sheet of glass, to renounce life in favour of television. One of them ingeniously levelled the barrier. NBC was legally prohibited from broadcasting *The Today Show*'s sound track into the street. A cashier in a Broadway restaurant, who joined the sidewalk audience every morning, therefore bought himself a portable set, which saved him from having to lip-read. Others knew that a debut outside the window was a propitious preliminary to climbing through that window into the box. The adolescent Dick Cavett, on his way from Nebraska to Yale, hastened on his first morning in New York to 49th Street where he stood among the crowd waiting to be recognised by the camera inside. He was blessed: the camera did absently idle across his face, and his family in Nebraska spotted him among the show's pavement public. He rejoiced as if his television career had already begun.

From its technological origins television inherited the responsibility of shrinking and thus harmonising the world. The CBS evening news broadcast began in New York, extended next to Boston, Philadelphia and Washington, and gradually filamented the continent, expanding south and west until in 1951 the coaxial cable allowed the programme to reach California. The news reader Douglas Edwards began his first bulletin by saluting the territory the medium had opened up for itself in an electronic resumption of the previous century's exploratory march across the continent to settle the far west: 'Good evening everyone, from coast to coast.' Television's demarcation of its air-space was accompanied by gestures like this one of heroic zeal and spiritual healing. The Beatles appeared on the first global telecast by satellite in 1967 to assure the world that all it needed was love. As those plans for *The Today Show* reveal, dominion of the air-waves seemed – at least to television's professionals – an advance towards the millennium. Television had set the world's sensorium tingling and ecstatically twanging. Houses raised antennae on their roofs to catch the fibrillations from the air. It all looked like a latterday version of grace irradiating the world and shivering into everyone's house by way of those rooftop conductors. Inevitably therefore the medium was coveted by evangelists, who take over Weaver's notion of televisual man as a communicator and welcome the air-waves as an empire of faith. They have adopted and grandiosely developed television's initial dream of the technological future.

Television has enabled Billy Graham to take the entire world as the theatre for his ministry. He can save souls on several continents simultaneously by means of a television link-up (and can blame the devil for any breakdowns in transmission). He planned his European mission in 1970 as a technological campaign. He would speak at Dortmund, from where his gospel would be beamed by microwave to Hamburg and then transmitted across Europe. Graham exulted at the prospect of universalising himself, conducting 'an all-European crusade by means of closed-circuit television'. He hoped to abolish frontiers at the same time as disarming obdurate wrongdoers. When national governments blocked his telecast, they convicted themselves of unregeneracy. The 1970 campaign was banned by Sweden, which declared closed-circuit television an offence against civil liberties. But Graham was gratified that Swedish Christians had crossed the Norwegian border to watch his programme. Yugoslavia, officially atheistic, quibbled by banning the direct relay from Dortmund but permitted videotapes to be shown later, imagining perhaps that Graham would be deprived of his salvific potency if his image wasn't carried live. The crusade was staged so as to identify redemption with an appearance on television. In cities connected with the relay, those volunteering to be saved made their commitment to a picture of Billy Graham glimmering ectoplasmically on a giant screen. More so than in person, elongated on this screen and projected like a spirit across frontiers, Graham didn't so much deputise for as embody God. Where Graham was present, the cameras recorded the decisions of those who came forward at his urging to be confirmed in their faith: the renewal of their lives began, for these people, with their television debuts.

Conversion signifies our receptivity: the person becomes an aerial, attuned to the invisible, spiritual currents of air. There have been other, more malign proposals for the use of television. Lyndon Johnson kept three sets in the presidential office, one for each of the networks, as if by simultaneously watching a variety of channels he could somehow tune himself into the mood of the refractory country he was trying to govern. Nixon, however, saw television as an instrument suited for the surveillance of a treacherous population, and toyed with the idea of fixing an electronic device to every American television set. The president could then switch on sets across the country in a time of crisis and use them to counsel or hector his subjects. Johnson had simply wanted to watch the country on those multiple screens, but Nixon's hope was to infiltrate the sets themselves. Though he was dissuaded, his idea had a certain symbolic propriety. He realised the set's power over us, its tendency to make an abject appliance of us. Television may plug us into the world, but we in turn have to plug ourselves into television. Disapproving social workers note the tendency of harried mothers to pacify troublesome children by sitting them in front of it, electronically subduing them. The American networks, testing viewer responses to their new shows, virtually wire their audiences to the set. CBS arm you with a pair of buttons, one red, the other green, which you push to signal approval or boredom; ABC and NBC sit you at a rheostat dial invidiously marked with a series of grades from 'very dull' to 'very good'; but some local stations employ television's equivalent of the polygraph, a test of galvanic skin response. Electrodes are attached to your fingers, and if you're emotionally roused by what you see, the voltage crackling on your skin is intensified. While the set is entreating you, you're responding to it in its own electrical idiom. The body can even be wired to take photographs as well as to transmit messages. For the moonshot in 1969 television cameras were built into the spacecraft, and Buzz Aldrin had a still camera in his breastplate so that, during his walk on the lunar surface, he could take pictures merely by pointing his body in the required direction.

Television manufactures people in its own technological image. Its characters are creatures who could exist only on television: they are residents of the box, whose faces are screens. A later chapter, commenting on television's detectives and private eyes, will contend that, because television is so two-dimensionally bland, favouring amiable anonymity, the only way it can ensure a character's individuality is to burden him with a tic, deface him with a quirk – Kojak's lolly-pop, Columbo's scruffy rain-coat, Rockford's beaten-up trailer. Similarly television breeds automata, prodigies whose special powers are (like the individualising disabilities of the detectives) mechanically or surgically implanted, as were the bionic organs into Lee Majors and Lindsay Wagner. Television's bogies are lab-concocted: an overdose of gamma radiation, we're informed, altered David Banner's body chemistry to metamorphose him into the incredible hulk. Television's extra-terrestrials are supernatural because they can technologically cut corners. Sally Field in *The Flying Nun* soared round Puerto Rico rectifying social abuses thanks to an aerodynamic cape, and Clark Kent when changing himself into Superman chose as his dressing room a phone booth, a cubicle which is the site of another technological miracle. The mental X-rays of Ray Walston on *My Favorite Martian*, which enabled him to eavesdrop on the thoughts of his suspicious neighbours, are no more than a refinement of that array of television screens in George Burns's den, which enabled him to monitor Gracie's mishaps elsewhere in the house. These are characters who cryptically celebrate television itself, which as technology is an extension of our feeble human powers. As the Martian, Ray Walston actually sported a pair of retractable antennae, like an indoor aerial squatting on top of a television set. He was rigged up as a human gadget: to raise his antennae, he pressed a hidden trigger to work the transistorised controls in his collar. He's a precursor of Big Bird on *The Muppet Show* who, like Aldrin on the moon, has a television set concealed in his feathery bulk so he can be manipulated from a distance. Julie Newmar as the robot in the situation comedy *My Living Doll* disguised her electronic workings as sexual equipment: her breasts were the casing for her solar batteries, and the beauty spots on her back were the camouflaged dials which gave access to her circuitry.

Wizardry on television is a magic conjuration of the millennium promised by the ads, when our lives will be blissful because we'll have appliances to rid us of our household cares. Samantha in *Bewitched* is a technological maven who can do the housework by remote control, at the twitch of a nose not the flick of a switch. Actually Elizabeth Montgomery on that show enjoyed the services of a troop of off-camera domestic servants, who performed the dirty work her magic affected to abolish. One of her tricks was to clean the kitchen by raising her arms and uttering a witchy formula. While she kept her arms suspended (which, she complained, was itself hard work), the cameras were turned off and the crew rushed in to dust and polish so the scene could continue. On another occasion, her suitcases packed themselves and carried themselves out of the house. But the chores which were Samantha's sleight-of-hand remained a drudgery for the special effects technician, who for this scene wired up the clothes and the cases and jerked them through the air from a parapet above the set. The misbehaving ghosts on another situation comedy of the 1950s, *Topper*, were rationalised as expensive mod cons. In this series, Topper (Leo G. Carroll) finds that his house is haunted by its two former residents and their St Bernard, which had perished with them under an avalanche on a skiing trip. The ghosts persecute the new tenant with their jests. One episode had them invisibly bathing their dog in the backyard. Seeing nothing but water cavorting of its own accord, Topper's wife was alarmed. He, in on the secret, calmed her by calling it 'our new sprinkling system'.

On television a genie, like these percolators the ads cheerily personalise as Mr Coffee, is a household help. *I Dream of Jeannie* teamed a bottle-bound female genie with an astronaut. He rescued her from her curse when he crash-landed on a Pacific island; she returned the favour by saving his life and signing on as his ductile personal slave. *My Living Doll* redeployed the same formula as sexual fantasy. Here Robert Cummings was a psychiatrist in charge of the sexy cybernaut played by Julie Newmar. On television the housewife has her arsenal of blenders and vacuum cleaners and dish washers to fulfil her affluent dreams. Why shouldn't a man's lusts be serviced technologically too? Television therefore invents Robert Cummings's robots and the airline stewardesses in a recent series of commercials who in requesting you to fly them were issuing a surrogate sexual invitation at the same time as touting their company's jets. Sexual innuendo on television is technological: hence those lewd Blic-flicking routines on behalf of cigarette lighters. Sex is a matter of switching on, plugging in, a mechanical incision of grooved and oiled parts. Bob Hope even saw in the set itself a body not, like Whitman's, electric, but excitably electronic. Admiring Jane Russell's cantilevered breasts, he invited her to join him in a new game called television: 'I'll turn your knobs and you watch my antenna grow.' The televisual antennae of Ray Walston's Martian were his means of surveillance, as if from a satellite like those through which television images are relayed; Bob Hope uses the antenna's erectile potentiality for a less enlightened purpose.

Family relations as well as sexual attraction were reconceived technologically by television. In 1965–6, the same season which inaugurated *I Dream of Jeannie*, NBC introduced another situation comedy entitled *My Mother the Car*. Jerry van Dyke acquires a 1928 vintage automobile and recognises the voice on its radio as his mother's: she has been reincarnated as a jalopy. Her crises are automotive. In one episode, as the car toils through the mountains in winter, mother gets drunk from the alcohol in her antifreeze. As a technological appliance, she demands the companionship of her peers. Another episode had her protesting about the miserable nights she had to spend alone in the garage: she demanded that her son buy her a television set. By such ingenious stratagems as these, the medium remakes us in its own image.

3
Medium

Cameras, though they pretend to be innocuously recording our reality, are all the while altering it by their mediation. They have their different styles of refraction. All of us wince in self-defence when a still camera is aimed at us: we know it will paralyse our faces, excerpt a static moment from our changeful existences, make a still life of us. When the shutter clicks, we're sentenced to death. Hence the sadness of old snapshots: those defunct selves are irrecoverable, and serve only to mock our present desuetude. The still camera is a grim archivist, memorialising the ages of man, snatching moments of happiness from us even as they occur by framing them and consigning them to the past. Movie cameras work differently, because the images they capture are mobile and, when projected, magically aggrandised. By drawing so close to the human face and then inflating it for inspection on a screen, the movie camera renders the face transparent. In front of the still camera we try to hide behind our faces, fixing for ourselves an armoured self-image. The movie camera won't be tricked by these evasions. It demands self-exposure, the mind's reflection in the face, and it studies the quirks of physiognomic expression as intently as if they constituted behaviour. Movie stars have entered into an intimate compact with the camera, permitting it to invade their consciousness, to be the confidential mirror in which they scrutinise themselves.

The television camera is different from both these, with its own definition of reality and its own etiquette of operation. Its special, sinister aptitudes are for intrusion and for reduction. Before television, the camera trained for its indiscreet work in other forms. The television camera's nasty propensity for catching people unawares or at a loss is prefigured by the newspaperman Weegee, whose uncovering of a blemished nocturnal New York in *Naked City* (1945) was later developed into a television series; the television camera's proclivity for espionage and the ferreting-out of the forbidden is prefigured in the cinema by Alfred Hitchcock.

Weegee toured the city after dark, searching for scenes of tenement arson or burglary or savage death to photograph. Most of his photographs were taken at night, but even when working by day he used a flash bulb. He had his technical reasons for doing so, but the choice is also a declaration of intent. The bulb's explosion startles the subject, and stalls him in its lurid glare. The camera is Weegee's weapon, the flash its ammunition. He can when necessary be more unobtrusive with his instrument, if stalking a prey which would be frightened off by the incandescence of the bulb. Gatecrashing Mrs Vanderbilt's opera party, he apologises unremorsefully to the male patrons of the Metropolitan who've been made to look ill-shaven and vulpine: 'It's really because of the invisible infra-red rays which bring out the hidden colour in the face.' After midnight at Coney Island he prowls the pitch-black beach, guessing at the positions of the lovers writhing there by the sound of their giggles and grunts, and aiming his camera to 'take a picture in the dark'. The lovers twine together, ignorant of the spy nearby; but generally Weegee delights in photographing a privacy which we see indignantly but helplessly protesting – felons, frogmarched by the police, hide their shame from the camera behind handkerchiefs or hats. When he photographs the arrest of a suspect who doesn't object to the camera, Weegee feels obliged to explain. The gentle old man tottering on a cane, who has just knifed to death a blonde in a hotel room, doesn't complain; but the reason is that 'he couldn't see my camera, because he was blind.'

Hitchcock's cameras are always peeping-toms or importunate keyhole-oglers, inveigling their way into recesses of prohibited knowledge. His cameramen, like the character played by James Stewart in *Rear Window*, adopt photographic spying as a prurient pastime, and develop it into a means of forensic detection. Hitchcock's films characteristically begin with the camera's demonstration of its sly manoeuvrability, as it penetrates a barred or shuttered room – vaulting the railings to peer in at the London flat in *Dial M for Murder*, swooping from mid-air to glide across the sill and under the blinds into the seamy Phoenix hotel room in *Psycho*. Sometimes, in these initial sequences of stealthy advance on the subject, Hitchcock includes the cameras which are his symbolic search-warrant. *Notorious* opens, in the antechamber of a Miami courtroom where a Nazi collaborator is being tried, with a shot of a newsman's flash camera waiting to pounce, then crosses the room to inch open the door and eavesdrop on the sentencing through a narrow slit. The film begins with the camera's deft negotiation of a closed door, and ends with a door resolutely and fatally shut, disbarring the camera, when Claude Rains walks back into the house to face the ire of his betrayed colleagues. For Hitchcock the camera is a device of paranoid inquisition. Like any weapon, it's a means both of assault and of defence: the assassin in *Foreign Correspondent* uses his camera as a cover for his gun; James Stewart in *Rear Window* fights off his assailant from his wheel chair by discharging volleys of flashbulbs like bullets.

These days the cameras are everywhere. The news teams daily shoulder their way down rooming-house corridors and follow the police into the apartments where murders have been committed, or aim their long-distance microphones over the heads of the crowd to listen to the *sotto voce* deliberations of the politicians. The camera's journalistic power is its adeptness at picking locks and easing open the doors of privilege. The fictionalised television account of Nixon's presidency was boastfully entitled *Washington: Behind Closed Doors*. Bombarded by the cameras, we've eventually managed to relax in front of them. The man in the street, his opinion solicited for a news item, is jovially ready to comply. The willingness of people to be accosted and interviewed is astonishing: we all apparently expect it, tolerating it as one of the irksome privileges of citizenship, like completing the census or doing jury duty. No one ever seems to tell the camera they're in a hurry or don't want to be bothered. We acknowledge the television camera's authority over us, and when detained by it are ready to assist it (as if it were the police) with its inquiries.

The television camera early on licensed itself to spy. This was the comic liberty claimed by Allen Funt's *Candid Camera*. Hiding the camera charged it with an alarming power, since it always caught us out, publicising our incompetence or our vanity or our panic. Funt's cheery injunction, 'Smile, you're on *Candid Camera*!' compels the victim to share in the joke. Maybe this is why the passers-by canvassed by the news programmes are so quick to deliver themselves of their opinions. They're appeasing the camera, which they know will otherwise turn against them. For the television camera has always been sneakily skilful at capturing things it's supposed not to see. The derisive candour of Allen Funt's camera later becomes a tactic for journalistic snooping. Michael Douglas's television camera, negligently slung under his arm but discreetly whirring, transcribes the nuclear accident in *The China Syndrome*; during the siege of the Iranian Embassy in London in 1980, a television camera in a suitcase was smuggled past the police barricades. The microphones which travel in tandem with the cameras are equally intrusive. Roone Arledge, when in charge of sports on the ABC network, inserted microphones into the shoulder-pads of footballers, and once planted a microphone under a zebra's carcase so it could record the grisly sound of the dead beast being eaten by a lion.

Television controls the people on whom it spies by scaling them down to fit its small screen. This is how it traduces the human face. Movies magnify physical features, metonymically isolating and enlarging a single expression or appendage and identifying the star with that part of him or herself. It segments the faces or bodies it's trained on, in order to fetishise them. The detachability of limbs and organs and expressions becomes an item in the mystique of movie stardom. Betty Grable *was* her legs, which Lloyd's insured for $1 million. The exigent camera demanded the rearrangement of faces before it would consent to photograph them. Jane Fonda when screentested was told she needed to have her jaw smashed, her teeth reset, her hair dyed and her breasts augmented. In exchange for this cosmetic martyrdom, the camera will confer beauty not only on the face but on its separate parts. Movie faces are so unreally huge that we remember separable features as insignias of character – Edward G. Robinson's sneering lower lip, the sullen gash of Joan Crawford's mouth, the quizzically asymmetrical eyebrows of Vivien Leigh. The movie camera has worked to make these people more than human. Television belittlingly makes its subjects less than human. The most expert television comedians are those who, knowing the camera will deface them, collaborate with it by making themselves extravagantly ugly. Hence the virtuoso face-pulling of Lucille Ball or Carol Burnett, or the maniacal mugging of Bruce Forsyth. Lucille Ball's scriptwriters had her repertory of grimaces codified – 'Puddling Up' for the face's collapse into tears, 'Light Bulb' for a look of crazed inspiration – and would simply insert the correct password in their stage directions, as if pressing a button to turn on the precise distortion they required. Television has enabled Phyllis Diller to make a career out of her shrill shrewish ugliness, and she likes to exhibit the surgical scars she's inflicted on herself to attract the camera's attention: she's had two face-lifts already, she recently bragged on Mike Douglas's talk show, and a third is scheduled. The slight tremors which enliven a face in the movies are lost on television. They can either be risibly exaggerated, as by the self-parodying comedians, or else smoothed out altogether, as by those immovably bland news anchormen, whose faces are the attestation of their probity and neutrality, refusing to react to the news they're transmitting. Ill-at-ease with people – either encouraging them comically to contort their faces or packaging them as personalities, wrapped in cellophane not human flesh – television perhaps is best with sub-human worlds. Animals come into their own when caged in the box. They match its scale, and the medium's candour enables it (as in David Attenborough's *Life on Earth*) to watch them without scruple, for they're not acting to impress it or feigning naturalness, as humans would. Likewise television caters to the eccentric and the introverted, those who have retreated into small worlds of their own mad devising. The BBC is forever reconnoitring such oddities – a retired military man zooming above the countryside in home-made autogyros, an amiably loony maths master in the series *Public School*. Television is good with reclusive obsession, with characters who, like David Attenborough's specimens, are snug in dwarfed worlds effectively the size of the screen. The NBC series *Real People* in auditioning the freaks who were its subjects took this mandate literally. Among its unreal real people were a family of midgets and a man who had constructed a banana-shaped space-ship, in which he intended to flee from nuclear war, accompanied by several thousand homunculi who had been protectively miniaturised to a height of one inch and were stored in baskets in his basement.

As at the Iranian Embassy siege, the television camera is expert at inveigling its way into areas which ought to be forbidden to it. During the siege it did so by subterfuge, but generally its technique is more insidiously ingratiatory. It encourages us to believe that it's our ally, and then when it's gained our trust it quietly defames us – or observes us defaming ourselves. We can't object to its betrayal of us, because we consented to allow it into our privacy. While professing sympathy or at least impartiality, the camera is all the while cynically interfering in the reality it examines. Its subjects must be willing to sacrifice themselves to it, like the Louds of Santa Barbara in the 1973 documentary *An American Family*. Their existence as a family was imperilled as soon as they invited the camera into their house, for its presence was a provocation. Aware that they were being studied, their relations with one another became strained and self-conscious. The camera expected them to supply it with indiscretions and antagonisms, and during the period in which the documentary was being made the parents divorced and their eldest son rejected them and declared his homosexuality. Though the camera affected unobtrusiveness, it had conspired to help make these things happen.

In watching programmes like this I've often wondered why people permit the cameras to witness their humiliation. Are we so vain as to imagine that the camera will persuade others to see us as we flatteringly see ourselves? Television actually ensures the opposite: we imagine that the inquisitive lens will see things our way; but it's detached from us, defining and deriding us as querulous, aggrieved objects. A couple of recent programmes illustrate the mistaken trust of television's victims in the camera as a means of justice and reparation, even as it's indicting them. One is the BBC's *Public School*, the other a backstage film about a telecast of Ponchielli's *La Gioconda* from the San Francisco Opera, shown on American public television.

Public School sums up the sad paradox of television's relation with those it calumniates. The school (Radley, near

Oxford) welcomed the series as a public relations exercise. It turned out quite differently: the headmaster is seen reciting pious platitudes to boys who are arrogant brats; the teachers, despairing, protect themselves inside their fads and harmless follies. One episode in particular reveals how the television camera encourages people to perform for its benefit and then, when they find themselves in trouble, coolly denies responsibility. A boy breaks the rules by driving his car into the school with a girlfriend to attend a dance. He's berated by a master, who won't allow him to drive home again with the girl and orders him to spend the night at school. The girl objects, quick-wittedly claiming that she has to go home to take some medicine and hoping to wheedle the boy's freedom this way. But the master frustrates this project by offering to drive her himself while her date remains in captivity. All this, with subsequent angry recriminations, is filmed, including a secret interlude in which another boy asks the girl, in confidence supposedly, if she really needs the medicine: they repair to another room to consult, but the camera pursues them. Everyone emerges murkily, the boy and girl as pert and smug, the master as a sorry drip. But the moral of the story concerns the culpability of the television crew. The boy, filmed driving his car into the quadrangle, obviously believed himself to be under the camera's protection. It can't be an offence against the rules, because it's all acting, a fiction enacted with the camera's connivance. Yet reality supervenes, and he's punished after all. The girl, arguing with the master, keeps insisting that the cameras were on him when the transgression occurred. He wouldn't, she says, have broken a rule knowingly: the cameras evince that he must have believed himself to be in the right. She might more logically have accused the cameramen – weren't they abetting the lapse by filming it? But she appeals to the camera as her saviour, unaware that it's now accusing her by recording her bleary-eyed tantrum.

Backstage in San Francisco, the camera is even more officious. It barges through closed doors: the crew lackadaisically pokes the camera into Norman Mittelmann's dressing room while he's costuming himself; he indignantly routs the intruders. It also brazenly publicises private scandals. Once more, those whom the camera is denouncing believe it to be their most staunchly partisan defender. At the end of the performance of *La Gioconda*, the soprano Renata Scotto, in a temper because she believes her colleague Pavarotti has monopolised the applause, won't appear on stage for a curtain call. She rudely dismisses a well-wisher who calls on her because he incautiously announces himself as a friend of Pavarotti, curses the audience and the upstart tenor it has preferred and promoted even though the opera (as she points out) is named after the character she plays. The stage director tries patiently to pacify her, telling her she's tired from overwork and assuring her that she's had a great success. The scene has all the illicit excitement of television, because we feel that we're eavesdropping, that the envenomed Scotto can't know that the camera is present – is it perhaps hidden in her closet? She sits at her dressing table and rages at her reflection in the bulb-framed mirror, with the contingent of appeasers behind her. She disdains to look at them directly, just as she ignores the camera, engrossed in her own narcissistic fit. Then, in her peroration, she does acknowledge the camera, not to scold it but to demand its allegiance. She threatens to quit San Francisco and leave behind her 'questa gente di merda'. Having said so, she turns to the camera and repeats the epithet with wagging finger: 'yes, *merda*, that is the word.' The camera, she assumes, is there to document her righteous ire, and she repeats herself to ensure it transcribes her Italian expletive correctly. She seems unaware that the camera is always a witness for the prosecution. Before the programme was broadcast, the producers screened it for Scotto, sure that she would object to their publicising of this dressing-room spat. But she couldn't understand their concern, and remarked that she thought she looked fine. It's this credulous vanity on which the camera so astutely practises: we're all loth to believe that it's not our friend.

The movie camera mystifies its subjects; television, as in these cases, scurrilously secularises and demeans them. This is why, during the 1950s, the movies so feared the new medium. It was an enemy to illusion, a debaser of sacrosanct cinematic images. The movies defended themselves against its ironic diminutions by hyper-inflation – wider screens, thronging spectacle, stereophonic sound – and by snickering asides. Half way through *Will Success Spoil Rock Hunter?* (a 1957 Cinemascope film) the action pauses, and Tony Randall, playing a writer of television jingles, delivers a snarling mono-logue for the benefit of television fans who crave interruptions. This alienatory device is seconded by a demonstration of the competing medium's technical deficiencies. While Randall expatiates on the virtues of television, the screen contracts to a fraction of itself, accidentally slices off Randall's head, fogs up or is blurred with streaky blizzards, before gratefully reverting to its full, cinematic size and steadiness.

Even after the end of these early hostilities, the relation between the movies and television continues to be quarrel-some. Television is the repository of the cinema's past, its untended graveyard. The studios auction off their archives to the networks as a gesture both of self-contempt and of scorn for television: it's the mediocrities, the movies no one wants to revive, which are junked, and in disposing of them the studios have condemned television, which above all venerates novelty and lives exclusively in the present, to the tedious self-repetition of reruns. In buying up the cinematic past, television in its turn made a cult out of the very obsolescence of these faded images, mocking them with campy tenderness. Tech-nical self-aggrandisement didn't help the movies, for black and white and the small screen came to constitute a style just at the moment that the coloured, widened screens of the 1950s made them redundant. We derived an aesthetic from those technical disadvantages, which had now been passed on to television. Hence the slick, sleazy glamour of *film noir*. We began to long for the grimy claustrophobia of the small screen and, when television caught up with the movies by acquiring colour, the most precious intervals were now those reserved for old black and white movies. Belying technical progress, we're now prepared to enjoy almost anything, so long as it's not in colour. Black and white vouches for age, and therefore for sentimental value. Style for us is whatever's perished, outmoded, lost. Television caters to this regression by resurrecting old movies and the old emotions which adhere to them. The threadbare fantasies of the late show are the perfect, mordant consolation for the insomniac. In the sleepless hours we confront our own extinct selves. To see again on television a film you saw on its first release is an odd and touching experience. Not only does the film date – it dates you. The difference in your response, always more critical the second time around, measures the disenchanting changes which you have undergone in the interim; and the difference is made more piquant by the fact that, the first time, you went out to see the film, whereas it now makes a house-call, returning in the night like a phantom to haunt you.

Television's tributes to the movies are always barbed. The annual Oscars ceremony, for instance, shames the sacred monsters of the big screen, fastening on them with unpitying confidentiality while they're at their tautest and most nervous. Television's triumph is to show that these illusory divinities are no different from the rest of us. Appearing on talk shows, the stars take care to register that they too are real people. The Oscars ceremony further testifies to their reality by depriving them of their competence. They lack the practised television personality's gift for improvisatory chatter – how badly most of these highly priced actors read the cue cards, how they stumble over foreign names, how unimpressive they are, banally thanking their families at the moment of their apotheosis. Televisually, the evening's spectacle consists in a demonstration of a dozen ways of clumsily failing to open an envelope at the first try. In becoming human, these people disappoint us. And though the Academy Awards presentation is about winning, television, hurtfully candid, prefers to dwell on the discomfiture of losing. One of its techniques, used during the 1980 ceremony, is to assemble on the screen a montage of the faces of nominees for the major awards while the envelope is being awkwardly ripped open. As each nominee is tabulated, his or her face is shown full screen, then relegated to a miniature and kept on hold in a corner until it's joined by the faces of all the others. The five hang there briefly together, suspended and in suspense. When the lucky name is announced, the expressions of the four losers are glimpsed for a moment, then the miniature of the winner reflates to full screen, obliterating the others. The technique exploits without mercy the competitive hysteria of the occasion. The heroic, impermeable faces of the cinema screen are first reduced to less than human size, then shown plagued by their own emotions, not the fictitious emotions of a character they're enacting. In 1980 Sally Field – who eventually won – and Bette Midler looked distraught with anxiety as the nominees for best actress were listed. Our lowlier instincts are excited by television's disrespect for privacy: when the winner is known our eyes leave him or her and flicker across the four dejected countenances before the camera deserts them; if we're quick enough we can watch them rearranging their looks of dismay into gallant smiles of congratulation for their victorious colleague. Johnny Carson, mischievously playing host in 1980, further snubbed the cinema's divinities by inventing a temporary celebrity of his own, as television is wont to do. He took as his subject an obscure sound technician who didn't appear to collect his award, and interrupted the proceeding whenever he had a chance to issue bulletins about the man's imaginary,

accident-prone progress to the hall where the awards were
being distributed.

At its beginnings, television made a bid for legitimacy by
attaching itself to state ceremony and even religious rite,
implying that the simultaneity of communication which its
technology made possible would enrol viewers everywhere in a
loyal community or a devout communion. In 1954 the coronation of Queen Elizabeth II and the beginning and end of her
Commonwealth tour were shown live on the BBC; in the same
year Pope Pius XII celebrated a mass at St Peter's on television,
and in doing so blessed the medium as an electronic extension
of the charmed circle of faith – 'May this first international
programme be a symbol of union between the nations'. The
conclaves of state obligingly rearranged themselves for the
cameras, amending protocol. Instead of ranging the opposite
factions in the 1954 Senate dispute between McCarthy and the
Army at different ends of the committee table, the antagonists
were seated side by side so they could share the television
screen. Camera angles became a matter of judicial etiquette:
the two teams changed places daily, to ensure that each had the
same ration of full-face and profile views.

Senator McCarthy, vilifying those he imagined to be traitors
in the televised sessions of the Committee on Un-American
Activities, made the camera itself a court of law, a photographic tribunal in which reputations not actions were tried
and physiognomic self-possession tested. But despite his
attempt to enlist the camera in his demagogic campaign,
television, knowing itself to be a belittler, turned against
political authority, and even against the rehearsed composure
of ceremony. The camera's special genius is for seeing what it
oughtn't to notice, for intrusion and levelling revelation. At a
ceremony, it prides itself on closing in on the domestic or
comically incongruous details which haven't been premedi-
tated. Even the staid British *Television Annual* for 1954
remembers from the coronation a succession of such acts of

televisual espionage: 'the newly crowned Queen's simple, white handbag, on the seat before her within the golden coach' or 'the inquisitive outreach of the young Prince Charles's hand to the golden Armill, still about the Queen's wrist, as they stood on the balcony.' In both cases television has diminished the pageant to a charade. The monarch is after all no more than a woman with a handbag, a mother with a restless child. Another recollection in the *Television Annual* thrusts the process further, showing the floundering of ceremony into a soggy shambles: the writer wistfully remembers 'the joyous defiance of pelting rain by Salote, Queen of Tonga, in her open carriage'. Aware of television's enthusiasm, as with the inundated Salote, for travesty and disarray, the British monarchy was and partly remains suspicious of it. At first the crowning in Westminster Abbey was to be broadcast on radio, not shown on television, though later the palace agreed to allow the cameras in. Why the original embargo? Insurance, perhaps, against the commission of a television indiscretion – what if the presiding archbishop had dropped the crown?

The White House early accustomed itself to television's democratic pushfulness. Truman led the cameras on a tour of the building in 1952. Thereafter the medium became convinced of its right of entry: perhaps its brashest assertion of this prerogative came when Barbara Walters in one of her interviews required Jimmy and Rosalyn Carter to tell her if they slept in the same bed. Those studious of their dignity, like the royal family, ration the liberties they permit to television. Only someone conscious of an inner vacuity, an unsureness of self, and longing to have his existence validated, would trust the cameras. Nixon did so, hoping to blackmail them into befriending him by offering them his tears, first in his Checkers speech, later in his maudlin farewell to the assembled White House staff. Like the tape machines which recorded the incoherent stream of his consciousness, television was of use to Nixon because it seemed, by reproducing him, to confer on him a magic unreality, licensing him (as in those calculated breakdowns over Checkers and Watergate) to simulate emotions of remorse or indignant innocent grief which he didn't feel. For him the exercise of power was cognate with this escape into an absolutist fiction. That's why his presidency at its most harried and paranoid became an act to which he hoped television would lend credence. He appeared, when making his mendacious presidential statements on the networks, elaborately supported by the insignias of office – his seal, an American flag on the desk. But this only served to further diminish his authority to a posture, as if he were inhabiting a frail set in a studio and not the Oval Office. Nixon indeed regarded himself as a member of an international confraternity of television performers. Meeting Prince Charles in London, he at once congratulated himself and ingratiated with the prince by saying, 'My daughters see you on television – and so do I.'

In the 1960s, half-heartedly proposing to democratise itself, the royal family selected television as the medium for its own measured desecration, and permitted the BBC to film its members earnestly joking at breakfast or frying sausages for a picnic. Television has encouraged the Queen to relax during her Christmas broadcasts to the Commonwealth. On radio, she used to enunciate an impersonal sermon. On television, she has gradually compromised with informality, no longer posed rigidly at her desk, even showing us her home movies. Some of the royal prohibitions, however, remain. The cameras are forbidden to show the monarch eating, and the American networks had to interrupt their coverage of the Washington banquet for the Queen in 1976 while food was being consumed (they were readmitted for the dancing). Why this taboo? The Queen presumably has impeccable table manners. The reason seems to be once more a fear of television's craving for indignity. The monarch has two bodies, one sacramental, the other merely corporeal, and the cameras, while professing reverence for the symbolic acts of the former, are actually more interested in watching the latter alimenting itself. In keeping the cameras outside, the guardians of protocol were warning that the occasion was a ceremony not a vulgar meal. But the media devised an adroit reprisal. If the eating couldn't be shown, then the preparation of the food would be, and one of the networks retained Jean Marsh, the parlourmaid from *Upstairs, Downstairs*, to describe it, thus resolving the courtly prohibition into a matter of repressive snobbery and, incidentally, making this bicentennial celebration of international accord an episode in a soap opera. Upstairs, the toffs were gormandising; television's place, which it confirmed with a vengeance when it engaged Jean Marsh, was downstairs, among the disrespectful scullions.

After the assassination of J. F. Kennedy, television assumed the responsibility of conducting the nation's mourning. By a unique self-denying ordinance, the networks banned ads and entertainment for the three-and-a-half days between the killing and the funeral. On this occasion the presence of the cameras wasn't defamatory. Rather, they were a cause of stoic self-control in the participants. Mrs Kennedy on the Friday had insisted on wearing her bloodied pink suit for the return flight from Dallas to Washington, so as to confront the cameras with the evidence of her husband's meaningless extinction. Having administered this televisual shock to the nation, she then cathartically relieved it and herself on the Monday during the procession to the Capitol. Once or twice the cameras caught her prompting the other tragic mummers – pressing her son, for instance, to salute the coffin as it passed. And during the eulogies in the rotunda, the cameras couldn't resist noting the truancies of human attention – an epidemic of coughing among the rheumy politicians, the fidgeting hands of the president's daughter. Mourning is an exercise in the solemn protraction of time, a reliance on formulaic responses as an escape from disabling personal emotion. It's not an event but an aftermath, a long and healing inquest. It's therefore ill-suited to television, and during the Kennedy funeral the medium's concentration did indeed falter. Television was forced to make an excruciating choice between the deliberation of ceremony and the casual, contingent violence of experience, to which it owes its first loyalty, for on Sunday, during preparations for the arrival of Kennedy's body at the rotunda, Oswald was gunned down on camera from Dallas. The networks had to decide whether to respect the ceremony or to disorder it for a newsflash from Dallas. It's often remarked that if, during the performance of a tragedy, a public execution was announced in the street outside, the theatre would instantly empty. Certainly the television cameramen would join the stampede. In 1968, NBC was arraigned for a similar televisual treason when, during its relay from the Chicago Democratic convention, it switched away from the speech seconding the nomination of Hubert Humphrey to show the rioting outside on Michigan Avenue, with Mayor Daley's police clubbing the anti-war demonstrators. By making this transfer, the network was thought to be intimating a partisan preference. The criticism was unfair. Television was merely, as during the Kennedy funeral, keeping faith with the nature of its medium, adhering to a messy, inflammatory happening rather than the stale, rehearsed routine of a political endorsement. All television cameras, not only Allen Funt's, are remorselessly and promiscuously candid.

4
Talk

On television, conversation has become a spectator sport. Merv Griffin, appealing for some opening volleys of applause from his studio audience, promises the crowd in the bleachers and the viewers at home that they'll 'meet my guests'. He means that we'll watch him meet them. The guests are invited to talk, but they accept in order to be seen: they belong to the repertory company of the professionally famous, the televisually known, who, having made themselves instantly recognisable, commute between Griffin's show and Mike Douglas's and Dinah Shore's, touting their latest film or album, or simply registering that they're still around. Television talk is not conversation but a celebration of visibility. Like the soaps or the games, it's a genre which has grown into an institution, stretching across the American schedules through the entire day, from Phil Donahue's earnest early morning therapeutic forum to Johnny Carson's satiric banter late at night.

The talk show is itself an oxymoron. What's showy about talk? The networks in the 1950s were suspicious of such programmes, insisting that television was a visual medium which had abandoned the loquacity of radio. It had to show things rather than tell them. On television, language is virtually a dirty word. The cable company Home Box Office, which presents recent feature films for its subscribers, has a code in its monthly brochure to warn customers against movies which might offend them, and one of its short-hand terms – along with 'nudity', 'profanity', 'adult situations' – is, simply, 'language'. It means foul language, but the abbreviation carries a televisual slur, implying that language itself is to blame. Television values an ad-libbing glibness with language, the capacity to run on inconsequentially and fill up dead air, but this is a different gift from articulacy. The sports commentator Howard Cosell is prized by his colleagues because he can chatter to order, on any subject and for however long might be needed. If you require 4 minutes and 20 seconds of noise, he'll provide precisely that. This is where tautology comes in handy, enabling you to rattle on while marking time mentally. I recently heard an announcer on American public television, appealing for donations from viewers, aver that 'these programmes are expensive – they cost a lot of money.' Another functionary of PBS, during an upstate New York station's campaign to round up contributions, threatened viewers with his filibustering fluency, delaying a feature film to repeat over and over again the categories of donation, means of payment, and the station's toll-free telephone number. He conceded that he was talking in order to wear us down: unless we all picked up our telephones to silence him by pledging to subsidise the station, there was no reason, he pointed out, why he shouldn't defer the movie indefinitely and go on repeating his message. This announcer had understood the logorrhoeal nature of television talking. Words are background noise, a repletion of silence, and also a whittling assault on the will. Mike Douglas, teasing replies out of tongue-tied guests on his talk show, relies on a litany of self-repetition, cajoling Bianca Jagger by assuring her 'You're known all over the world – you're known internationally.' The duplication had its own poetic aptness: the fact that she is known is the only thing there is to know about Bianca Jagger; she's the epitome of the talk show guest, famous not for anything she's done but because she's talked about and because she's visible. Douglas doesn't trust a statement unless he's made it twice, for safety's sake. Later in this same interview he raised the subject of the jet set, inquiring what changes Bianca Jagger had noticed 'in that style of life – in that life-style'.

Since television needs din and drivel, it's a mark of special continence and fortitude of spirit to remain quiet while the cameras are on you. Ronald Reagan, having won the Republican nomination at Detroit, established his spiritual credentials by making just such an audacious gesture. In preparation for the electioneering 'crusade' (as he called it) ahead, he asked his audience to observe a moment's silence. Not, be it noted, a minute's – that would have been too exorbitant a waste of network time, a graveyard of stifled air. During the appointed moment, Reagen's face puckered in devout concentration Then, looking up, he remarked 'God bless America'. It was an act of startling temerity, identifying benediction with the silencing of television.

Talk on television isn't meant to be listened to. The words merely gain for us the time to look at the talker. The talk shows are theatres of behaviour, not dialogues. Richard Burton, a guest on Dick Cavett's show during the summer of 1980, admitted that whenever he watched talk shows his attention was always monopolised by the footwear of the participants. Crossing their legs, the talkers aim their shoes at the camera. To illustrate the point, and in response to Cavett's query about his superstitious habit of always wearing some article of red, Burton unzipped his boots and removed them to place in exhibition a pair of multicoloured socks. The camera, taken aback, avoided his feet for the rest of the exchange with Cavett, but Burton had neatly succeeded in demonstrating that the talking was secondary to the showing.

Valerie Perrine appeared as Merv Griffin's guest during September 1980. They began with some desultory talk about her current movies, after which she wandered offstage to return with four oversized, wolfish dogs. Sitting, staying, slobbering over their mistress or responding to Merv's mocking yaps, these dogs constituted our entertainment for the next ten minutes, until they could be ushered off under cover of a commercial. The audience meanwhile obliged with mirthful approbation. Watching, I wondered why the dogs were considered to be funny. They were just dogs after all, not doing tricks but slumping on the plastic studio floor or prowling lazily about. They weren't acting; they were behaving. But because the talk show is a theatre of behaviour, the dogs, once admitted to it, automatically became entertaining. The fact that this segment of the show could sustain itself for so long with no words except the host's canine yelps and his guest's giggles at her family of pets revealed how inessential talk is to the talk show – and even, perhaps, how dispensable is the element of show, for the dogs were enjoyed precisely because they weren't putting on a show. Things on television don't have to mean anything: we just require them to be there. The more contingent and unconsecutive they are, the better. Dick Cavett prides himself on avoiding obvious topics with his guests, just to see what will happen if he asks an unanticipated or irrelevant question, and Johnny Carson derives a more antic, aleatory comedy from his awareness of television's truth to the way life improvisatorily happens. One night in 1977 Kenneth Tynan watched Carson on a whim discard his expensive scripts, littering the floor with commissioned jests and making vertiginous comedy from his very lack of preparation. This is why Carson's straight man Ed McMahon, the uncomplaining object of his jokes, is so necessary to his act. McMahon can be heard off camera, during their supposed dialogue at Carson's desk, eagerly agreeing with everything his master says, bravely trying to keep up though never sure what Carson will do or say next. How appropriate is the salaam with which McMahon greets Carson at the beginning of each show. Every one of Carson's acts is for McMahon an act of God – arbitrary, inexplicable, unrepeatable, and very often mean. It's this inspired randomness which makes Carson one of television's geniuses, and one of the medium's self-images.

Because the talk shows are about visual witness not the bartering of ideas and opinions, a virtuoso like Carson can afford to ignore or disdain his guests, his face glazing over with boredom or his eyes widening in disbelief as he darts the visual equivalent of an aside into the camera which is reserved throughout *The Tonight Show* for close-ups of his reactions. The guests are engaged so that Carson can react to them, beckoning us to join him in the wry act of looking. In a television interview the drama is likewise visual not verbal. The interviewer's aim is not to elicit a spoken answer to a question but to provoke a self-betraying facial reaction from the subject. We don't listen to what the politicians are saying, but scrutinise their faces for evidence of their discomfiture, and marvel at their composure and their poker-player's skill at physiognomic lying. It's these televisual standards which have made 'credibility' the measure of probity in politics. Credibility means the integrity of your visual image. It's a cosmetic scruple: in the 1980 presidential contest the newsmen were fond of arguing about whether Reagan dyed his glossy hair, as if the veracity of his coiffure were an ethical issue. To be credible doesn't necessarily mean to be truthful. Rather it means acting as if you believed in what you're saying, the ability, when interrogated by the camera, to make a mask of your own face. In retaliation, television interviewers have developed a nagging and hortatory style, asking impertinent questions in the hope of extorting a giveaway grimace. Mike Wallace on his ABC interview programme used to grill his subjects, demanding of a male milliner why the rag trade was so homosexual an avocation, or else reprove them, informing Grace Metalious that he considered *Peyton Place* low and carnal; John Freeman on the BBC's *Face to Face* conducted an unforgiving moral examination of his guests, in some cases reducing them to tears.

Even when the show's format is one of amiable chat, the host is likely to ask questions of ghoulish tactlessness. In the winter of 1980 Kenneth Tynan made his last appearance on Dick Cavett's show. Shortly afterwards he died of pulmonary emphysema; already he was emaciated and breathless, his lungs ruined by chain-smoking. During the interview he fumbled for a cigarette and haltingly lighted it to relieve the physical strain of his gasping talk. Cavett, after temporarily demurring because he suspected that his guest 'might not want to talk about this', remarked that the last time Tynan was on the show he'd been trying to give up smoking – what progress had he made? Tynan's death-rattle of shock and disbelief was the protest of every persecuted talk show guest: 'Is a man to be spared nothing? Is no area of privacy sacred?' Not even mortal illness is respected by these cheery inquisitors. Dinah Shore is adept at enticing the 'friends' who are her guests to confide in her about their erotic dreams and specifications. 'What first attracted you to your girlfriend?' she asked Tom Wopat of *The Dukes of Hazzard*. 'I could really embarrass myself here,' replied her nonplussed friend. She encouraged him, and in doing so propounded a charter of liberties for her prurient medium: 'That's what TV is for. Let it all hang out.' Later on she continued her genial attack, asking 'Are you going to get married?' and adding unremorsefully, 'I'm very nosey.' Wopat collaborated without complaint, assuring her that it was her business to be nosey.

The most pryingly aggressive of television's inquisitors is Barbara Walters of ABC. Her interviews are harangues. Richard Pryor is berated for his sexual, alcoholic and narcotic misdemeanours, John Derek for his nympholeptic manipulation of his young wife Bo. Alan Alda is ordered to tell whether he ever 'cheats' on his wife, Laurence Olivier rebuked for his prosaic description of himself as a worker ('God',

Olivier muttered in retort, 'is a worker'). Barbara Walters prides herself on having castigated her subjects and lashed them into submission. Friends, she brags to Pryor, congratulated her on her treatment of him in a previous interview, saying 'Boy, did you show him!' Interviewing Jimmy Carter in October 1980, she obtained a confession by iterative force. She began by informing him that he'd made a tactical error in vilifying Reagan, and issued a warning that in subsequent weeks he'd have 'to get back on the track again'. Carter agreed, smiling wanly. 'No more name-calling?' she persisted, requiring a promise from her refractory subject. 'I'll try to do better,' said Carter. 'Mr President,' she rejoined, sensing triumph, 'are you apologising?' Carter, hoping he wouldn't have to grovel, said he preferred to call it 'explaining'. But Walters refused to be rebuffed, and asked her question – on behalf of pitiless television – over again: was he admitting that he had been wrong in deriding Reagan? 'Yes, I will say that,' said Carter, wearily acquiescing in her attack and pleading guilty. Though on this occasion Walters was professing shock at the muck-raking conduct of the presidential campaign and demanding that Carter make amends to her, within three weeks she had altered her position. Her televisual responsibility is to embarrass her victims into self-revelation. She doesn't imagine that they'll own up to the crimes with which she charges them. Generally they slither aside or else, like Bette Midler, comically order her from the house. Her aim is to excite those twinges of shame or disgust we see on their faces. Carter's apology was an unexpected bonus, which is why she had to insist on his repeating it. Therefore, at the end of October in the presidential television debate from Cleveland, she put to the two candidates a question which belied her previous affectation of horror at their slanging-matches. During the debate, Carter and Reagan had treated each other with studious courtesy. Walters proposed that they should abandon gentlemanly decency, and invited each to say why we should not vote for the other, and why his election would be harmful to the country. To make it clear that she wanted them to engage in the personal recrimination she had earlier reproved, she asked each candidate to define the 'greatest weakness' of his opponent.

The Walters manner of shrewish scolding is the conversational equivalent of the television camera's unflattering intimacy. Celebrities offer themselves to the interviewer in order to be humanised – which, on television, means to be demeaned. The talk show is a machine for reduction. Appearing with Mike Douglas in August 1980, the opera singer Roberta Peters briskly put herself through the talk show's course in self-devaluation. She despatched an aria, chattered brightly, then offered to exhibit the trim body ('size 6', she noted, defining herself in consumer terms) which is the secret, she said, of her vocal longevity. Stripping to a leotard, she skipped rope, challenged Douglas to do the same, and then to advertise the firmness of her diaphragm (which supports the voice) stretched herself prone on the floor and requested a fellow guest to stand on her stomach. This led to an orgy of exchanges: soon everyone was poised atop everyone else's diaphragm.

The chair on which the talk show guest squirms is a vinyl pillory. The audiences know how to play the reductive game, and when they're permitted to join in the questioning they ruthlessly deprive the celebrity (whom they're supposed to admire) of his secrets, and at the same time of his mystique, embarrassing him into equality with them. Recently, again on Mike Douglas's show, Chad Everett withstood such a free-for-all. Each question from the audience was designed to make him flinch – 'Do you wear pyjamas in bed?' or 'What was the most embarrassing thing you ever got caught doing?' or 'Can I have a kiss?' Douglas himself enjoys pruriently coaxing trade secrets from his guests. Bruce Dern, for instance, was asked to tell whether he 'got excited' during a nude scene he'd filmed with Ann-Margret. Dern conceded that there had been a problem. He had debated the issue in advance, wondering 'if I got excited would it scare her, and if I didn't would it offend her?'

On Douglas's show or in Barbara Walters's interviews, these intrusions can seem salacious or overbearingly ill-mannered. But they're to be blamed on the medium, not on the individuals who are its agents. Television has no respect for persons: in surrendering yourself to the camera, you forfeit your privacy. On Phil Donahue's early morning talk show, however, this televisual theft of our personal psychological property is benignly therapeutic. Donahue's show is a forum, a problem-sharing and problem-solving democracy. The guests aren't roped off on a remote stage but sit among the studio audience. The format is that of the encounter group. As always, the celebrities divest themselves of aura and exclusiveness, showing they're no different from the audience. Betty Ford comes on to talk not about being First Lady but about being a reformed alcoholic, Marsha Mason to discuss her Indian meditations not her acting. Yet, as managed by Donahue, this intimacy isn't improper or denigratory but communal and participatory. The programme testifies to a faith that everything can be overcome by being talked out, pooled, exposed to the cameras. The audience can ask questions and so can viewers, by telephoning in. The television set becomes a confessional, offering to those who submit themselves to its chastening investigations a sense of purgation which is almost religious. Donahue is not the first to employ the medium for absolution. Some of television's failures have abjectly begged the box's pardon. When his show was floundering, Jerry Lewis, catching sight of a priest in the studio audience, called for the last rites; and Jackie Gleason, after his game show *You're in the Picture* failed ignominiously, took over the last episode in the series to express his regret, sitting on a bare stage explaining why the preceding programmes had been so vile.

In February 1980 one of Donahue's programmes dealt with obesity. His guests were women who had lost weight and written books about dieting and the spiritual well-being they derived from their new slimness. They acted as confidantes and comforters to the women in the audience, many of whom admitted that they'd believed they would suddenly become happy and beautiful if they could lose 30 pounds, only to discover, when they'd shed that lumber of flesh, that they were still miserable. Redemption is Donahue's business. In this case the recipe for the attainment of bliss is perfection of the body; other programmes purvey psychiatric dekinking of the brain or (when Marsha Mason appeared) a meditative calming of anxieties. Donahue himself, with his Catholic upbringing and his prematurely grey thatch, is a priestly character, who in pleading with his interviewees to tell him the truth implies that he's doing so for their own good. He fails when he encounters a hardened sinner who won't own up to remorse or even to vulnerability – as, for instance, with Truman Capote. Donahue pleaded with Capote to admit that, despite his armature of drawling scorn, he was insecure and perplexed. Capote testily refused to yield. He wouldn't apologise for himself, which is what Donahue's therapeutic forum required. 'Are you comfortable with your own persona?' Donahue demanded. Capote declared that indeed he was. 'Then why do I feel so uneasy?' wailed Donahue, who felt uneasy precisely because he'd failed to make his guest recant. Donahue recruits his psychiatric freaks (including, a while ago, an inveterate flasher and his put-upon wife) and maimed artists and then delivers them to the studio audience – a jury composed, he says, of 'the finest folk you'll find in America' – to receive their absolution or condemnation. But Capote wouldn't accept the verdict of the assembled housewives. 'Are you always this nervous?' one of them asked with maternal solicitude. 'I'm not nervous at all,' Capote snapped, twitching the while. Donahue implored him – on behalf of all those watching who were too short or too tall, of all those women who were too thin or too fat, who weren't like the glossy magazines told them they ought to be – to offer up his own private terrors as a gift to aid his fellow sufferers. Still Capote wouldn't be budged from his self-possession. In desperation, Donahue invoked that more threatening majority of which the studio audience was a benevolent sample: what about all those brawny truckdrivers who must want to exterminate so 'profoundly effeminate' a person as Capote? Didn't that prospect alarm him? 'That's their problem,' pouted Capote, defying the massed and mobilised truckdrivers of America.

Donahue has sanctified the talk show's inquisitiveness, and made it a technique for spiritual alleviation and psychiatric ministry. Transcripts of each programme are available at a cost of $2.50: the dialogue is intended as a do-it-yourself kit, to be taken home and used for self-readjustment. Some of his viewers expect him to provide medical services. One old lady sent in a cheque for $3, beseeching Donahue to prescribe a reliable laxative. Yet this sacred trust has licensed him to probe further than his licentious competitors into matters formerly private and guarded by taboo. His programme has filmed an abortion and a child-birth.

The peculiar oddity and televisual inauthenticity of the talk show lies in its vacillation between talk and show – talk which rambles on unrehearsed between friends, and a show in which people archly tell one another things they already know in order to amuse an eavesdropping audience. Dick Cavett sometimes makes a private joke from this fraudulence, for instance asking the baritone Sherrill Milnes, whom he's interviewing, 'Will you sing something for us?' and mocking the simulation of spontaneity – the vocal numbers have been agreed on and rehearsed, with a pianist in waiting – by adding, 'I think I know the answer – at least I hope it's still the same.' Though these conversations pretend to be taking place in a living room, their actual location is the television studio. The sets for the

American shows masquerade as domestic nooks, but are always metamorphosing into glossy, brassy stages. Dinah Shore converses in a simulacrum of a suburban living room, with occasional tables and cups of coffee (never touched) surrounding her and the friends who seem simply to have dropped in on the way past. Guests do sometimes wander in unannounced, as if on a brief errand to borrow a cup of sugar. When Beverly Sills was Dinah Shore's guest, Carol Burnett – on business, presumably, elsewhere in the studio – appeared to do obeisance and then absented herself. But Dinah's convivial living space is apt to disassemble itself. A partition will slide away, to reveal a surprise guest in hiding (on one occasion the grandmother from *The Waltons*, victim of a recent stroke) as if in a closet; or, more bemusingly, a wall may suddenly turn transparent to reveal Donna Summer with her rock group in attendance – perhaps these are Dinah's boisterous new neighbours, making a din in the adjoining yard? And hovering out of view are the injunctions to the studio audience – fairground signs encircled with bulbs which flash on to trigger applause – belying the programme's affectation that it is private chat.

On Mike Douglas's show in the afternoon, the unexpected dilations of the domestic space in which the conversation is supposed to be taking place are even more startling and contradictory. Douglas lines up his guests in a motley row and hosts a raunchy party. Whereas Dinah's guests are genteel callers from the neighbourhood, Mike Douglas's are revellers invited so they can do tricks, tell lewd stories, engage in drinking contests and kissing games, or mount one another's diaphragms. Dinah is visited by social equals (the rich Dina Merrill, for instance, who brings – Dinah tells us – 'class into the room with her'), Mike by a rowdier crew of party-goers. Bianca Jagger, telling him about her return visits to Nicaragua, blithely remarked 'I went back for the earthquake,' as if that too had been a festivity on the jet set's agenda. Douglas's conversational space therefore tends to erupt into a theatre, with variety acts and a noisy band. The studio confines him, and he regularly abandons it, to broadcast from the lobby of a Dallas hotel (where he presides over a chug-a-lug tournament), the galley of a jumbo jet, or a Hawaiian resort. The show's itinerary makes Douglas himself one of those international sensation-seekers he admires, a fellow traveller of Bianca Jagger's: off he will trundle to Monaco for a film première. For him the conversational format is a device to connect a succession of star turns.

Dinah domesticates the studio. If her province is the living room, her competitors commandeer other portions of this fictitious house. Merv Griffin's programme is recorded in Hollywood on Vine Street, and one of the sets it uses has as its back wall a pot-planted terrace surveying a view of Los Angeles from the hills. The studio of course is windowless, the view only a photograph. But the pretence is important, for it suggests that Griffin's dialogues take place in one of those glassy bungalows jutting from the Hollywood hills, and that he is summoning his fellow luminaries from the level expanse of the city below up to this eyrie of panoptic privilege. Griffin has seized the room with the costliest, most megalomaniac view; Dick Cavett settles for the den. His studio is bachelorishly simple, unfurnished except for a pair of bucket chairs. His audience, though heard, is never seen. The pretence in his case is of unbuttoned camaraderie. There's seldom more than one guest, whereas his competitors end their programmes with a semicircle of gatecrashers. Cavett, as if to signal that this is not a public performance but backstage causerie, wears no tie. It's this exclusion of the public which explains that question about Tynan's smoking – acceptable, if the two were talking in private, as an indirect inquiry about a friend's health; tasteless only when mentioned before that invisible audience which a few minutes earlier had been chuckling at Tynan's jokes.

Donahue is unique among this cadre of comperes in not decorating his studio as a room. But he has in his own way subtly fictionalised it. Its starkness – ranks of chairs, a carpeted ledge for the guests, who aren't raised above floor level and thereby designated as performers – makes his studio a consulting room or perhaps a village hall, a neutral space hired for a meeting. Donahue is a member of the audience, sharing its dubeity, its eagerness to learn, and its deference. On a programme with Gerald and Betty Ford, he proudly displayed a copy of a Detroit newspaper prematurely headlining the expected Reagan–Ford ticket, which he'd had autographed. He doesn't play the host, entertaining guests in a replica of his own home. The guests, ensconced on their ledge, are the residents, and he's merely one of the importunate drop-ins.

The oddest set belongs to Johnny Carson. He begins as a showman, posed for his monologue of one-liners in front of a curtain, which defines him as a stand-up comedian. There follows a turn in costume: Carson attired as a soothsayer, or perhaps as a garrulous rooster. Then the showman changes to talker, and repairs to sit at a desk. Next to this is a chair, occupied first by the self-effacing Ed McMahon, then by each guest in turn. To one side is a sofa, the disposal area for used and discarded guests. This layout cunningly deploys the forces with which Carson prosecutes his comic warfare. He has a desk to protect him like a bunker, his guests only a chair to writhe and fidget in. He occupies the desk throughout, since it is his post of command, but the guests are shunted from the chair to the limbo of the sofa, moved – after their fifteen minutes of celebrity – off towards the wings and tape-erasing oblivion. Carson is fiercely proprietorial about the desk and its accoutrements, which are the emblems of his power. Among them, as Tynan recalls in his profile of Carson, was a cigarette box, which Don Rickles smashed one night while substituting for Carson. As soon as Carson returned to the show, he spotted the damage. He at once sought out Rickles – who was filming a comedy series in an adjoining studio – and, trailed by a disconcerted *Tonight Show* camera, left his own set to break in on Rickles's performance, demanding, Tynan says, 'both reparation and an apology'. The story illustrates not only Carson's superstitious self-investment in the props scattered on that desk (they confer reality and permanence on him: 'that's an heirloom', he said of the cigarette box, 'I've had it for nine years'; they can also, as Rickles discovered, become comic weapons) but also his wicked disrespect for illusion. He knows the studio is just that, and because he's never deceived by his own illusion he delights in interrupting and demolishing the illusions of others, as he did by walking into the middle of Rickles's comedy routine. Likewise he relishes gags which misfire, because he can then slip out of his own act, grimace at the material his writers have served up to him, and tell the audience, 'Yea, you were right about that one.'

The suppositious room in which Carson receives his interviewees is half domestic, half official. The guests imagine they're in a friend's living room; but Carson, impregnable behind that desk, isn't relaxing with them. He is at work, as if in his office, and for him talk isn't casually amiable but an astringently competitive business. The room's cryptic uncertainty about its own identity is complicated by the false wall behind the furniture. For years this was a rustic photograph of a lake surrounded by pines, in alienatory contradiction to the room which it closes off. Was the mural an affectionate homage to the middle America from which the Nebraskan Carson originates and which supplies him with his following, or was it a jibe at the interior decor of the suburban homes in which the programme is being watched? Its implausibility seemed deliberate and ingenious. The room is unreal, a pseudo-place rigged up in a television studio. The studio is in Burbank, but the view from its fake window is an expanse of mid-western forest. The unreality is the essence of Carson's treacherous style, for he knows how to exploit to his own ironic advantage the special inauthenticity of the talk show's format. He lures these people into his house, only to aim a camera at them. He encourages them to divagate and digress, and then with a smirk in close up betrays their trust by acknowledging that he at least knows they're on television, though they may not have suspected it. The other talk show hosts are pained by the unreality of feigning a tête-à-tête under arc lights, in front of cameras and a studio audience of unwelcome strangers, but Carson derives a special power from his witty acceptance of the medium's alienation effects. For instance, the host, when he makes his first appearance, has to smile through a chorus of cheers and whistles from the audience. Carson, never at a loss, responds by semaphorically conducting the applause, his arms in constant motion as he stands there. During his monologue he regularly needs to glance down at the cue-cards beside the camera to check on his next joke. Rather than concealing his dependence on the cues, he exploits it: those sneakily averted eyes have become one of his comic expressions, a grin of complicity as he prides himself on his possession of this hidden script and the calculated appearance of spontaneity it makes possible. The small errors and dead-ends of conversation don't perturb him. If he makes a mistake in introducing a guest, he will shuffle the information sheets on his desk and confess with wise weariness that after you've been doing a show like this for a number of years the pages of notes (like the people to whom they refer) become indistinguishable. Carson's quick-wittedness engages him in a rivalry with the camera, and this is the essence of television style: trained permanently on him, the lens defies him to keep going, daring him to invent new quiddities of gesture and expression, to find ways of overcoming the dullness or inanity of the guests who are sent out to him; and he always manages to do so.

In September 1980 Carson got a new set, the old hunting lodge having been declared unsalvageably tacky, and in the course of introducing these refurbished premises he once more experimented with their unreality. The mid-western lake and forest have been superseded by a Los Angeles penthouse, with a painted view of the horizontal city at night. Carson ordered some close ups of the new carpets and the new curtain before which he delivers his monologue, paid tribute to NBC's interior decorator, and then went on to deconstruct this fictitious place. He pointed out the fallacies in the mock-up of a view. It couldn't be seen from the *Tonight Show* studio, which is on the wrong side of Hollywood hills: one of Carson's alienatory jabs is to insist that, though the show is advertised as coming from Hollywood, it's actually taped in Burbank. The appurtenances of the new set, Carson remarks, were imported from a bordello in Barcelona. He distrusts the new desk with which he's been issued, because he doesn't yet feel he owns it: he riffles sceptically through its drawers. Spying a door, he's determined to open it, speculating on the possibility of speedy exits on nights when he has boring guests. There's nothing behind the door, but he pretends he's found the men's room.

Though Carson exults in these unrealities, Dick Cavett is at his most disarmingly apologetic when reminded that the private talk in which he's engrossed is also a public show. After his initial introduction of his guest, he only addresses the audience to warn them that they're privileged eavesdroppers on someone else's conversation. When the free-associating talk is responsible for some serendipity of phrasing or imagery, he is apt to tell the audience, more or less indignantly, that 'we didn't rehearse this': in the act of recognising the audience's presence, he's denying that the conversation is staged for that audience's benefit. This is not, he's declaring, a show. Nothing could be further from Carson's manner. He always conspires with the audience (which means with the camera) against the unfortunate guest. Cavett admits the unreality of the format only to ask pardon for it. Terminating the conversation when the half-hour of air-time is up is always a problem for him, since here the show supervenes to arrest the talk. Cavett resigns himself to this with charming awkwardness.

Sometimes he even looks to the side of the camera and, startled, says 'Good night' – explaining to his guest that one of the crew has just held up a cue-card emblazoned with those words, so the abruptness of the guillotining is no fault of his.

Other hosts are less scrupulous. They know the talk is simulation, and rely on the recurrent commercial interruptions to ease them out of difficulties. Jack Paar on *The Tonight Show* once asked Miss Miller, the elderly devotee who was in the audience for most of his tapings and who has since transferred her custom to Merv Griffin, why she turned up so often. He no doubt expected a compliment. Instead Miss Miller's desolating reply was 'Because I'm lonely'. Paar's only recourse was to appeal in desperation for a commercial. In this instance, as so often on television, the ad was a relief from the programme, not the other way about. Donahue too uses the ads to snub antagonistic audience-members or incoherent phone-callers. Some programmes rely on musical euphemism to cushion these transitions from talk to commercial. On Dinah Shore's show, a discreet piano-underscoring signals that it's time for a break. Dinah occasionally draws the warning into the conversation by humming along with it; but despite the politeness of the musical hint, if a guest ignores it and continues to chatter the piano will swell to censor and submerge the voices. Carson, however, welcomes the opportunity to draw attention to these artificial foreclosures, because in doing so he's establishing his own superior acumen at the unreal game of talking on television. Tony Randall, one of Carson's line-up in August 1980, had embarked on a long and obviously rehearsed after-dinner story only to be halted by a tinkling chime from Carson's band, the cue for a commercial. Randall's reaction was a spasm of petulant rage. The chimes had ruined his exposition. He pointed out that he'd been air-freighted from New York, at considerable cost, to tell his stories, and now found himself stupidly up-staged by the ads. Couldn't Carson overrule those chimes? Carson of course would do no such thing. 'Listen,' he explained with grim patience, 'if it weren't for those chimes, you wouldn't be here telling your stories, and I wouldn't be here listening to them.' His protest quashed, Randall had to submit. The rejoinder was typical of Carson, in its formalistic bravura and in its cynicism. He's aware that he's on television, and doesn't pretend to be anywhere else. So televisual a man is he that he even conceives of his own extinction as a pause for a commercial: asked what he'd like his epitaph to be, he'll reply 'I'll be right back.' With Randall, he was both indicating the limits of the artifice he inhabits and rebuking a presumptuous guest by reminding him that the show itself is merely a bait to attract commercial revenues, its ratings guaranteeing the advertisers a clientele for their wares. How fatuous of Randall to imagine that anyone wanted to hear his stories, Carson was implying. The talk on both sides was purely mercenary. Randall was there earning his fee, Carson his salary, the network its commission, the advertisers their profits from sales.

Carson was right to point out the flimsiness of the form. The talk show, combining two incompatible elements, is possible only because of the devious mock-reality of television. If a guest arrived in the studio determined to treat it as the room it pretends to be, and to treat his interviewer as his host, confusion would ensue. Ralph Richardson did precisely this, in a spirit of reckless experimentation, when appearing on Russell Harty's talk show in London in 1975 (I owe the story to Tynan's *Show People*). Bumbling into the studio, Richardson at once dumbfounded Harty by assessing its decor, complimenting him on the 'very nice place' he inhabited and marvelling at its size. Like Carson opening that false door, Richardson peeped curiously behind the curtains which concealed the wall of the studio, and descanted on the imaginary view: 'you could see anything from here, couldn't you – the Tower of London, Buckingham Palace, the Post Office Tower? I'll bet you could.' The cameras he appraised as furniture or as gambolling domestic pets: 'You've got a lot more cameras in your place than I've got in mine. . . . Of course, you know them. You probably feed them. What do they eat? Celluloid and chips?' The studio audience likewise changed, as soon as Richardson spotted its presence, from a gathering of Harty's fans to a hostile jury: 'You've got a lot more friends than I have. Are they friends of yours? Or are they enemies? Shall I address them? Ladies and gentlemen of the jury, I assure you that this man Harty is innocent.' Harty gaped as the frail illusions on which his programme was based were toppled by this comic rampage. For once, the medium's bluff had been called.

5
Soap

Soap and sentimentality belong in partnership: both are selling the notion of a world cleansed of grime and fault, a world renovated by that cleanliness which is the sublunary equivalent of godliness. The alliance between the cosmic optimist and the launderer, which leads at last to television soap opera, begins with the Victorians. In 1886 Barratt the soap manufacturer acquired Millais's picture *Bubbles*, which has a scrubbed and chubby youth blowing at a soapy pipe, and used it to advertise Pears soap. The artist protested, but the picture and the product deserved each other. The meretricious gloss of paint as Millais applies it coats and varnishes surfaces. Victorian sentiment, correspondingly, trusts that all problems lurk safely on the surface, and thus can be expunged with a charitable smile or a lathering of soap.

Another Victorian manufacturing philanthropist, Lever, bought a domestic painting by Frith called *The New Frock* and used it to promote a brand of soap he called Sunlight. Frith's little girl proudly displays a dazzling garment. Lever attached to the picture her admiring testimonial: 'So clean'. This commercialisation of the genre painting was not cynical but messianically hopeful. Lever was devoutly concerned with the reform of social iniquity. However, for him the solution was to be moral amelioration not political change, and this is why soap can do duty as a symbol of his paternalistic schemes. Sentimentality defuses revolutionary ire, and can even glibly imply that it's the aggrieved poor who are to blame, not their plutocratic masters: they're the dirty ones, encrusted in soot and mud, and in issuing soap to them Lever is demanding that they make atonement by cleaning themselves up.

Between this Victorian wishful thinking and the psychiatric sagas of daytime television there is, admittedly, a difference. The Victorians were dealing with a society externally besmirched. For its soiling inequities, soap was, they thought, remedy enough. Our soap operas have renounced social conscience and graduated to the study of mental misery – that rankling discontent which is a luxury of the leisured, moneyed middle classes. Everyone in the soap operas is laved and deodorised, but despite this they're still unhappy. New cures are needed, and accordingly Victorian soap yields to those zealous powders and detergents – devised to cope, as the ads insist, with 'today's tough stains', with the ingrowing, introverted anguish of modernity – commended on the American daytime serials.

One of the pictures Lever wanted to buy for use in his advertising campaign was Stanhope Forbes's *Health of the Bride*, and he suggested to the artist that the wedding scene should be amended to serve his purpose. Instead of a glass, the best man who is toasting the newlyweds should be armed with a bar of soap and avowing 'Happy is the Bride that Sunlight Soap shines upon'. It's an unwittingly eloquent slogan. For the Victorians, soap can shine: charged with a sentimental mission in the world, purveying redemption along with disinfection, it's radiant, effulgent, effusive, sunny. In *Bubbles* it's exhaled as a medium of dreamy fantasy. But ours is a therapeutic age, in which the foamy benevolence of sentimentality no longer avails. Our problems aren't to be solved by wishing them away but by scientific method and mental incision. Thus there is a tacit accord between the American soap operas, preoccupied with neurosis and psychological grief or sexual torment, and the caustic, corrosive substances which vanquish dirt in the ads. Rather than interrupting the programmes, the ads complete them: they propose, with blithe illogic, chemical remedies for moral maladies, as if the gnawing purity of ammonia could ease your suffering at the same time as cleaning your stove. The puritan labour of virtuous cleansing has been magically eased by these lemony liquids and scouring powders, which do the work of fighting grease and filth on your behalf. But anxiety remains. These new products aren't only technological time-savers and problem-solvers: they create problems for their baffled domestic users. Their operation is surgical. They scratch and scar while at their abrasive work, and their fervour is dangerous. They're to be handled, we're always warned, with care and trepidation. They can consume your enamel and singe your plastic. This mortal world is too tender for their alarming fanaticism. They turn the kitchen and bathroom into laboratories and battlefields, operating-rooms or psychiatric offices, for, like the psychiatrist, they aim to strip and flay, to denude us of the protective pretences which are our integument. The Victorian soaps could banish dirt by smiling at or through it. The genial heat of sentimentality made problems evaporate. But the modern products are killers. They hound bacteria and destroy dirt, or lure roaches into a concentration camp disguised as a hospitable motel, from which, we're told, 'they won't check out'.

The mood of the American soap operas is stricken and morbid. They're about the quiet despair of the suburbs, where the technological abolition of material cares has only made room for a new despotism of spiritual and carnal incubi. They offer a tragic alternative to the compulsory cheeriness of the situation comedies which occupy the nocturnal schedules. The sitcoms are about the cohesion and enlargement of families. *The Brady Bunch* married Robert Reed, already equipped with three sons, to Florence Henderson, who had her own complement of three daughters. The title of another sitcom nonchalantly decides that *Eight is Enough*. Even Archie Bunker (the American version of Alf Garnett) is a patriarch, whose bigotry is pardoned by the indulgent affection of his kin: the programme, *Till Death Do Us Part*, transplanted to the New York suburbs, is reassuringly entitled *All in the Family*. Behind these suburban broods lies that most extended and tribal of all television dynasties, the Waltons. The schedules refer to the time-slot in which these programmes are housed as 'the family hour', and the description fits both the shows and their audience. The sitcoms celebrate the family's regroupment at the end of the day. They are therefore a world of snug mergers, in which the reassembly of the family watching the show is mimicked on the screen by conciliatory family alliances. Sitcom families are forever replenishing themselves, recruiting new members. Not even divorce sunders these cosy units: when Felix Unger and Oscar Madison are discarded by their wives, they set up housekeeping together as *The Odd Couple*. The widowed mother of *The Partridge Family* looks after a flock of five, which in 1977 was united for a single episode with the motherless family of *My Three Sons*. A family sentiment united even the bickering colleagues of the television newsroom on *The Mary Tyler Moore Show*. When in the final series the family was disbanded Mary delivered a moist-eyed eulogy which pays tribute to the spirit of situation comedy, with its conviction of the emotional safety of our dependence on one another – 'I thought about something last night: what is a family? And I think I know. A family is people who make you feel less alone and really loved. Thank you for being my family.' When the time allotted to the sitcoms by the schedules runs out, the set itself admonishes us to call the roll of our own family. 'It's 10 p.m.', the American announcers advise, 'and do you know where *your* children are?' Or, they censoriously inquire, 'Have you hugged your child today?'

These are nocturnal palliatives. The afternoon soaps are meant to be watched in solitude, not communally, and they offer to their house-bound female viewers a bleak training in the solution of the problems which stagger home in the evening – adulterous or alcoholic husbands, menaced at the office by predatory career women; dropped-out or drug-addicted offspring; meddlesome matriarchs. The family in the soap operas is a compendium of mental disquiets and sexual antagonisms. 'I'm trying to get thing straight in my head,' moans a beleaguered character on *The Young and the Restless*, engaged in sexual combat with her daughter for possession of the man they both claim to love. The secret, subversive hope of the soap operas – a libel on the marital joys of the sitcoms – is for dissolution of the enchaining family, and the absurder stratagems of their plots yearningly act out this dream. Both husbands and offspring can be disowned with impunity. That's why the soaps so often have recourse to bigamy and illegitimacy. Ben Harper in *Love of Life* was jailed for the former offence. In *Days of Our Lives* Michael Horton, jr, discovers that his uncle is his father; Brooke Hamilton turns out to be Bob Anderson's natural daughter; Rebecca North Le Clare, artificially inseminated, produces a son who's ignorant of his father's identity. The parentage of children can be, as in these cases, glibly reassigned. For spouses – if the contract can't be invalidated by the exposure of bigamy – the soaps propose other measures. Since marital sex is regarded as an infliction, the wives, like Susan Peters in *Days of Our Lives* and Felicia Lamont in *Love of Life*, have retreated into angry frigidity. For them, submission equals ravishment. When John Wyatt's mistress in *Search for Tomorrow* wanted to reclaim him from his wife, she telephoned him pretending that a rapist had broken into her apartment and beseeching his help. He went to her rescue, and was of course cajoled into passing the night there. The aforementioned frigid Felicia in *Love of Life* mistook her husband for a rapist and promptly shot him. A

conundrum in medical ethics becomes on the soaps a con-
venient means of terminating marital agony. Dr Seneca
Beaulac of *Ryan's Hope* switched off his wife's life-support
system, and Liz Foster did the same to her expiring husband in
The Young and the Restless.

The soaps entertain these malign dreams of disconnection,
but know there is to be no actual deliverance. The defining
characteristic of the soap opera is after all its mournful,
unassuageable continuity – its torturing protraction of time
(since everything on the soaps takes so tantalisingly long to
happen), its recurrence from day to day. The soaps aren't a
relief from the domestic routine which oppresses their viewers
but a confirmation of it: watching them becomes another
unshirkable daily chore. The soaps are occupiers of vacant
time, and as their titles suggest they have made their own
remorseless tedium into a cosmic principle. One of them is
called *As the World Turns*; introducing another, the lugubrious voice of Macdonald Carey declares that 'as sands
through an hourglass, so are the days of our lives'. The title of
One Life to Live makes existence itself sound like a dreary
domestic grind – an indentured expanse of time which must
somehow be passed, or killed.

The endlessness of the soaps is both their companionable
solace and their horror. Their rhythm of purgatorial prolongation makes them a replica of domestic boredom and a
chimerical escape from it. The genius of the form is its capacity
to dilate into whatever quantity of time it has to fill. In this the
soaps exactly parallel the nature of office-work, as Parkinson's
law defined it. The makers of the British serial *Crossroads*, set
at a motel, are expert at contriving meaningless action which
serves merely to keep the cameras turning and the viewer's eye
open until each episode reaches its statutory length. If an
instalment is a few seconds short, a scene at the motel desk is
added, with a guest signing the register or a staff member
taking an otiose phone call. Nothing of significance occurs, but

time has been triumphantly consumed, which is after all the form's promise to its viewers. Characters sometimes struggle against the enervating endlessness which is the life-sentence of the soaps. Occasionally *As the World Turns* rouses people from their paralysed misery and compels them to believe in the future or to start a new life. But these optimistic initiatives are contradicted by the wearying persistence of the series itself. Life on the soaps is just one featureless day after another. One of them is entitled *Search for Tomorrow*, but in the soap world tomorrow never comes, precisely because, when it does come, all it contains is another instalment of today, impeded by a recap of the non-events on yesterday's episode.

It's this which distinguishes the soaps from drama. Action in drama is a trajectory, abbreviated in time, confined in space, arching from a wilful beginning to a necessary end. Every moment in a drama has to be, as Aristotle insisted, fatal, because it advances towards crisis and conclusion. Drama is predestinate. But the principle of the soaps is the opposite one of deferment and postponement – not action but the filibustering frustration of action, the prohibition of an end. The soaps virtually arrest the time in which they're supposed to move, becalming us in an endless afternoon. Even the talk is decelerated. On the soaps, in contrast with the banter and chatter of the sitcoms, people converse with mesmeric slowness, expanding their words to fill as much time as possible. The theme tunes sag rhythmically, dragging towards musical slow motion. The soaps are embarrassed by the stray dramatic action which manages to get committed in their idyllically uneventful world. *Crossroads* spent long weeks framing the amiably oafish farm boy Benny for a murder of which he was not guilty, and then untangled the plot in a few bathetic seconds. The perfunctoriness seemed deliberate – a snub to action, to events, to happenings, to anything with the temerity to disturb the monotony of life at the motel. Not even death, the unavoidable dramatic ending, is permitted to supervene. Arthur

Brownlow on *Crossroads* was a while ago given a few months to live. He passed them with noble forbearance, waiting like everyone else on the soaps for the mercy of an ending, only to come across his own death-notice in the paper. Investigating, he discovered that the hospital computer had confused his diagnostic tests with those of another patient bearing the same name. He'd been issued with the wrong results, and was not due to die after all. As soon as he was reprieved, he was dropped for a time from the programme. He'd vanished not into the grave but into limbo, that forgetful, indifferent other world which lies outside the perpetual present tense of the soaps. Eventually he returned: for a while, however, he enjoyed that suspended, undead existence of absent soap characters, whose names are still invoked and who still occasionally make phone calls to the living. The continuity of the soaps is itself a cure for mortal ailments. Rachel Ames, who plays Audrey in *General Hospital*, began with a contract for three months, at the end of which she was to die. But once she established her usefulness to the show, her disease relented. 'I had lymphoma,' she comments, 'but I went into remission.'

Instead of the propulsion and sequence which are the imperatives of drama, the soaps favour the different time of habit and recurrence. Here they're learning from their medium. Time on television is rotatory – the same jingles in the ads, repeated until we've subliminally learned them and, when next in the supermarket, somnambulistically buy them; the same signature-tunes; the same listings week after week. Time's pressure to unravel ahead is stilled on the soaps, or reversed by the device of recapitulation. An actor in *As the World Turns* once had an 8½-page monologue in which, he marvels, 'I recapped my *entire life*!' However, even the past on the soaps is no more than conveniently time-killing repetition. Marooned in their torpid present, the soaps have as little reverence for the past as they have trust in the future. This is why they are so fond of amnesiacally erasing the past. Sooner or later, everyone on the soaps mislays their memory. Meg Mortimer, sovereign lady of *Crossroads*, found that amnesia was the quick way out of a plot complication. When the husband who had tried to poison her was reported dead in a car crash somewhere in South America, she got herself engaged to another suitor, only to find that her yet-living spouse had returned. She lost her memory until the divorce could be finalised. On *Days of Our Lives* the doctors, however inadvertently, have perfected a technique of amputating the memory. Amanda had an operation for a brain tumor. The conscientious surgeon relieved her of her memory along with her malignancy. Another heroine, Kim Dixon on *As the World Turns*, had her memory blown away in a tornado. Amnesia immunises the soap characters against the dramatic necessity of reaction. Temporarily lobotomising them, it enables them not to respond to the crises in which they find themselves. Nicole from *The Edge of Night* was the victim of a political bombing. Her husband, fondly fancying her dead, consoled himself elsewhere. Nicole then returned as from the dead, but blessed with memory-loss, unsure of her feelings, scrubbed clean of her history and therefore of her character. Depriving people of their pasts, amnesia acclimatises them to soap opera's charmed indeterminancy. They're saved from the obligation to act or react because they don't know who they are. They've been mentally set adrift in that sleepwalking stasis to which soap opera itself aspires.

The soaps beautifully equate form and content, medium and message. The conditions of their production are also the determinants of their peculiar world. They're not only interminable, they're actually about the drab infinity of domestic routine. The amnesia they visit on their characters both caters to the whim of actors and scriptwriters (allowing motiveless re-routings of the plot) and corresponds to their conviction of our secret longing to wander out of our lives, to disburden ourselves of family and of nagging, tiresome personal identity.

The soaps are a world of fidgety existential dubiety, in which a multitude of happenings – of arbitrary and inane comings and goings – covers the absence of anything which in drama would qualify as action: a resolution of the will, a purposeful expenditure of energy. Soap characters abhor a decision. On *Crossroads* it takes people months to decide whether to fall in love, or get engaged, or marry, and then in most cases they panic in extremity and do nothing. How many of the paraplegic Sandy's romances were aborted? Most of the action in the soaps must be credited to the scenery. Entrances and exits, opening and closing doors, are our relief, and a relief too for the incarcerated characters, who long for someone to arrive to divert them in their immobilised misery. Here, too, form and content overlap. Nothing ever occurs on the soaps, because the writers have parsimoniously to eke out events, distending them over as many episodes as possible; but this procrastination is true to the helplessness which the programmes are both alleviating and reinforcing – the doomed isolation of the housewife, who pines for the ring of the telephone or the doorbell to rescue her from claustration. No wonder the chimes in the 'Avon calling!' ad are the notes of emotional uplift. Now at last the door will open, someone will arrive, and there'll be a brief respite from this life of solitary confinement in the company of one's mod cons. In the cramped *Crossroads* studio in Birmingham, shoddy sets abut on one another: sections of cheap rooms in which the characters are penned, and which exhausted directors and cameramen try to expand by adopting odd angles or shooting through windows. Because the programme cabins us in this flimsy prison, where life morosely divides itself between a series of places which familiarity has made contemptible, a new set is greeted by us as by the characters as an access of liberty, as if a new room had been built onto our own house. The producers of *Crossroads* refuse to grant funds for exterior filming, and because the programme is locked in the studio the occasional outdoor sequences are exhilarating spells during which we're unleashed, and the eye is allowed to wander at will over objects which are dazingly strange to it. Content is true to the vicissitudes of form.

For their own opportunistic reasons, the soaps are a world of transience. Actors are apt to move on to more satisfactory jobs, and will need to be written out. Sometimes they die, and have to be retroactively provided with a plausible reason for doing so. At other times they're summarily executed. The American soaps are sometimes euphemistically said to be passing through a period of 'transition'. This means a purge, as new writers exterminate the characters invented by the previous team. But from all these compromises the soaps salvage a certain truth. They embrace this extraneous necessity and turn it to their advantage, for the life they represent is one of temporariness and instability, where no relationship can be relied on to last, where people are liable to drift inexplicably away or disconcertingly to reappear (like Meg's homicidal consort) after they've been safely forgotten. Since this is their view of things, the settings the soaps favour are places of transit, institutions through which people pass or are (like data in a bureaucratic system) processed, but in which no one belongs: a motel (*Crossroads*), a bar (*Ryan's Hope*), a pub or a corner shop (*Coronation Street*), a hospital (*The Doctors* or *General Hospital*). This choice of places suggests another adjustment of content to form, for the real location of the soaps is not these way-stations but the television set itself. In June 1980, *Coronation Street* celebrated its two thousandth episode, and in doing so made clear that it was commemorating not the programme's history but the set which contained the programme. Mrs Walker, landlady of the pub, announced the twenty-seventh anniversary of the Coronation, in honour of which the street had been rechristened. This homage to the monarchy was at once deflected into praise of television. Mrs Walker proprietorially remembered watching the ceremony on her set, which had been 'the first in this area'. But when she recalled how colourful it had been, she was corrected by the officious char, Mrs Ogden, who pointed out that in those days transmission was in black and white only, and pedantically quoted the date on which colour television began. The programme's history and the nation's disappear into the self-absorbed and self-celebrating box.

If the soaps are about a world in transit, that is because the television set is a place of transit. Destined sooner or later to wear out, it meanwhile wears out the people and information it exploits. Images flicker across its fickle stage and atomise, as we watch, into a fog of coloured particles. The medium, like the people in the soaps, lives exclusively in the present. The shame-faced abbreviation 'rpt' in the schedules is its admission of failure. Television has succeeded in making its own amnesia contagious. From the first, television-watching implied forgetfulness, remissness, dereliction of domestic or conversational or educational duty. Those who are watching the box are playing truant from the other things they ought to be doing. Television conspires to make us live through it. We're now plugged into the community rather than participating in it. We elect a government and then watch it govern us on television. The terms of our association with one another have been redefined by the medium, so that television founds its own community, in which the previous night's viewing on the box is the experience we all share. The parodic soap opera *Mary Hartman, Mary Hartman* made television the only society to which the zombified Mary acknowledged a connection. The show's joke was to make the characters behave as if they knew they were on television, so that their most casual conversation was carefully explicit exposition. Someone would refer to Martha, whose position in the clan would then be elaborately established by people who knew it already. 'Martha – you mean Mary's mother?' 'Yes,' would come the reply, 'and Tom's mother-in-law.' The box not only supplied Mary Hartman with her reality but proposed itself as a monitor of her mental health. In one episode her husband Tom pleaded with her to recognise that 'this is not a TV show'. He was wrong, as she enjoyed pointing out: their life was a daytime serial. Mary's mental collapse not only happened on television (while she was making a guest appearance with David Susskind) but resembled the breakdown of a television set. Like a guttering, imploded television tube, her mind began to emit bursts of mad static, advertising jingles and patriotic war-cries.

The viewer nowadays is the citizen. If he doesn't watch the box, he's outlawed from the society of his fellows and will have nothing to talk about at work tomorrow. He may even be suspected of mental recusancy. Mary can only officially return to mental health if she qualifies anew as a pacified and uncomplaining viewer. In the psychiatric ward she's told that she will be discharged if she consents to sit and gape at the television set, which will 'show them that you are normal'. Television confers normality and confraternity on its acolytes. The drop-in bars, motels or hospitals of the soaps are substitutes for the television set: like it, they're communities not of natural association but of electronic election and passage. Among the admirers of *Crossroads* are some who, obedient to Mary Hartmann's logic, would willingly exchange their reality for the programme's fiction and go to live at the motel – which means to take up residence in the snug cell of the television set. One such volunteer internee (specifying 'age 66½') wrote to reprove me when I criticised the serial in a newspaper column, declaring that 'one would happily reside at Crossroads'. For all their implausibility and incompetence, there's a disarming verisimilitude to the soaps: they may not be like life, but they're like television.

They also tell unsettling truths about the societies they represent. The American soaps are fables of individual self-development, of mental schism and recovery. *The Doctors*, the announcer asserts, is 'dedicated to the brotherhood of heal-

ing'. The English soaps, however, are fables of social reconcile-
ment. Characters are embedded in family and society, not
embarked on the American adventures of self-laceration
which impel the people in *All My Children* or *Days of Our
Lives* to abandon their spouses and seek their own therapeutic
salvation. The American soaps have adapted puritanism from
a religious to a psychiatric ideology. Tom and Alice Horton in
Days of Our Lives are God-fearing tribal elders, and though
one of their offspring has retreated to a convent, the other
junior characters belong in a new generation which sees the
cure of souls as a medical not a spiritual concern. No such
self-rending modern psychic quests trouble the English soaps.
They're about antique, feudal societies, whether in the York-
shire countryside of *Emmerdale Farm* or in the fraternal slum
of *Coronation Street. Crossroads,* with its motel-full of travelling salesmen near industrial Birmingham, conscientiously
establishes its own pastoral lineage. The motel is allegedly
located in a gossipily friendly village. Though the rural setting
is never seen, it's essential to the programme's pretence. The
motel is an extension of its proprietor's family home, and Mrs
Mortimer, despite this initial compromise with commerce,
retains a manorial and matriarchal responsibility for her
employees, bountifully queening it over a society which,
though it services those travelling salesmen who are the ad-
vance-runners of consumer capitalism, seems still rooted in an
agricultural dark age: the farms which supply the motel with
its produce are tenanted by revenants from a remote past, like
the muddy-booted yokel Benny or the Bible-quoting Reg
Cotterill.

Rather than psychiatric self-identity, the English soaps are
preoccupied with social cohesion, about which they're patro-
nisingly conservative. *Coronation Street* reconstitutes a defunct social class – an impoverished but jolly proletariat, content to subsist in picturesque squalor so long as it can afford
cigarettes and beer. *Crossroads* deals with the connected plight

of the imperilled but gallant middle class. Meg has to turn her home into a business; in the village the retired naval captain Ted Hope has had to open a shop. He sells antiques, merchandising a past he can no longer afford to own. But this foundering class retrieves some self-respect by making a value out of its own shabby gentility. Ted Hope's pedantry about the pedigree of articles in his shop is a rebuke to his customers, who are vulgar enough still to have money. He's particularly scornful of Americans. At the motel too they deal with the ambiguous strangers who are their customers by quizzing them about their occupation and trying to relegate them to their correct social place. The motel register aspires to the condition of a social almanac, arbitrating on the respectability of those whose names are entered in it. The flashy new beau collected by Mrs Mortimer on a cruise ship says he's a grocer, but everyone notices that he's too well-dressed for that – 'and have you seen his car?'

The tiered plots of the English soaps are, as in Victorian novels, models of social hierarchy. Mrs Mortimer's role as guardian of social law and communal hostess is duplicated in *Coronation Street* by the endearingly pompous Mrs Walker, who regulates the manners and morals of her staff and clients from behind the bar of her pub. Wealth, if suddenly acquired rather than being inherited (in which case it has been progressively diminished so as to strand its legatee anyway in the lower middle class), upsets this hierarchy. Therefore, whereas money on the American soaps is a necessary endowment, subsidising those lives of self-scourging idleness and psychiatric solipsism with which the programmes are concerned, on the English soaps it's dreaded and reprobated. On *Crossroads* the most alarming psychological hazard is the angry bewilderment of finding yourself ejected from your social class by unearned riches. Jim Baines the uncouth garage mechanic was ruined by his pools win. Swathed in silk kimonos and manacled with gross gold chains, he actually moved into the motel, impiously graduating from employee to client, and was soon after banished from the show. One of Mrs Mortimer's partners, David Hunter, suffered a temporary moral collapse after joining a Birmingham gambling club; another partner, Adam Chance (tinctured with a gambler's untrustworthy name), was made unscrupulous by his property speculations; Chris Hunter cynically wed a waitress to qualify for a legacy left by his grandmother; the rich Hugh Mortimer was kidnapped for ransom by terrorists.

Since the aim of these programmes is to derive a victory from economic failure, it's interesting that their way of killing the time each episode takes is to show people who, though supposedly at work, are engaged in precisely the same activity of listlessly whiling away time. Television itself is a beneficent time-waster, a device to ease us through the dreariness of duration, and the English soaps show characters inventively coping with this televisual predicament, managing to be on the job without actually working. *Crossroads* has its tea-breaks in the staff-room or coffee-breaks in the managerial sitting-room, *Coronation Street* its lunch-hours in the pub. Much of our time in watching *Crossroads* and *Coronation Street* is spent in the same way – not in observing action or attending to dialogue but in listening to orders for drinks or watching keys being handed over at the motel desk, activities as time-absorbingly futile, for us, as those the characters are meandering through. This temporal attrition, which is our bond with the characters, tells us something important about television; it also tells us a depressing truth about the society which produces and treasures these programmes, for England is a country in which industrial action has come to mean its opposite – no industry, no action.

In America such inactivity changes from an economic malady into a luxury, the highest stage of affluence which is leisure time when you're free to be yourself, relieved from the need to labour or forage for food. The riches which in the

British programmes disorient people are on American television a gift of grace, a grant of time to be expended on introspection. The millionaires in *Dallas* or *Executive Suite* are chronically miserable, but it's not their money which has made them so. They're loaded with wealth so they can luxuriate in their unhappiness. Outgrowing material cares, they've advanced to a new world in which their only anxieties are spiritual or psychological. Money in the American romantic tradition always inaugurates a career of self-discovery. Henry James's plutocrats redeem their grubby lucre by using it to finance tours of Europe which are their moral and aesthetic education. For Fitzgerald's Gatsby, romantic fantasy is synonymous with purchasing-power. Money enables you to actualise your dreams, to afford a new version of yourself (with a wardrobe to dress the invention in).

This American alliance between romanticism and capitalism explains the connection between the soap operas and the ads after which they're named. The serials show people grappling with the puzzles of personal identity, striving, as an earlier romantic generation said, to attain a soul; the ads translate this exorbitant romantic self-expectation into spendthrift consumerism. You are, the ads imply, what you buy, and you can change your life (as James's Verver or Gatsby did) by spending your money. Every commodity is a packaged promise, a vendible vision. The people of the serials are mired in doubt and guilt; the detergent ads rescue them by encouraging a psychiatric drill of self-laundering. Viewers refuse – and rightly so – to discriminate between the serials and the commercials. The presenters of the lavish *Another World* regularly get letters from viewers asking where they can buy the furniture or curtains used on the show. As well as coveting the props, viewers donate them. Gifts sent in for a marriage on *Search for Tomorrow* did duty as wedding presents in the relevant episode. Even the puritanical self-analysis of the characters tends to effloresce into self-indulgent romantic consumerism. An inveterate sufferer on *Days of Our Lives* was once told that he gobbled up therapists 'like a kid goes through a box of Cracker Jacks'.

The soap ads, true to the psychiatric vocation of the soaps, turn the kitchen into a consulting-room, the laundry into a confessional. Jane Austen's heroine in *Northanger Abbey* is dismayed when, in place of the narrative of woe and cruelty she believes she's found in her cabinet, she reads a prosaic inventory of domestic linen, enumerating shirts, stockings, cravats and waistcoats. But she's wrong to be disappointed by this washing-bill. Our grimiest secrets are after all confided to our linen. Desdemona was incriminated by a handkerchief. The proverbial prohibition against washing your dirty linen in public equates stains with secrets. Joan Blondell, the laundress slaving at the ironing-board in Busby Berkeley's *Dames* (1934), makes love to her clients at one safe remove by tenderly handling the under-garments they send her, and admits, after cataloguing and caressing the varieties of long-johns and pyjamas, that 'when I'm home on Sundays / I miss all these undies.' She teases and fondles the clothes as she hangs them out to dry and (jerked from above by wires) they respond, clasping at her with their linen limbs and chorusing that 'our hope is / you're pure as the soap is.' The laundry tempts her to these intimacies, enabling her to decipher the bodies of the wearers from the evidence of their casing, but supplies her with a moral alibi: her job is to cleanse and starch the concupiscent undies. The soap operas similarly guarantee to absolve you of your psychic stains if only you'll share them. At a town-meeting in *Days of Our Lives* a character agrees that 'we all have problems' but says, 'if we tackle these problems together they can be overcome.' The meeting is thus a communal psychiatric couch. On the serials people compulsively tell their secrets because they long to rid themselves of their gnawing guilt, and the ads make laundering an analogy for this obsession with self-purging. This is why such cosmic claims can be made for the detergents. A new product is advertised as 'a landmark in laundry history', as if the laundry was the setting for an evolutionary battle, in the course of which seamy humanity gradually purifies itself and prepares for the millennium inaugurated by those lightning-flashes of chemical radiance which assault us from the detergent packets.

Because the ads are small parables of puritan redemption and romantic self-renovation, in which characters erase the corruption which adheres to them and exult in an ecstatic cleanliness, they're infused both with the moral repugnance of the puritan and the emotional exhilaration of the romantic. You have to love cleanliness, and trust to it to invigorate and elate you. The kitchen is a combat zone between chores we despise and products we adore because they'll do the job for us. An ad commends Mop-and-Glo to those who '*hate* waxing', and a housewife converted to the use of April-fresh Downey for her laundry shrills 'I *love* that smell!' Identifying the product not with the task it performs but with the emotion it excites in its beatified owner, a dish-washing liquid has actually adopted the brand-name Joy. The ad shows it at its work, earning a housewife the bliss of being complimented on her dishes. This is the lyrical, romantic bonus of consumerism; another brand-name glances at the theological victory which underlies the emotion – a variety of oil which does battle with grease while frying chicken is proudly labelled Puritan.

As armaments in a modern, therapeutic version of the ancient puritan resistance to filth and degeneracy, these innocuous household products are promoted in a language of startling belligerence. The kitchen and the bathroom-cabinet are arsenals. Every item stocked there is a fighter, preferably a killer. An anthropomorphised demon spot-maker lurks in your dish-washer: blue crystals of calgonite will exterminate him. Sunflower oil in cooking 'fights' cholesterol, fluoristan in toothpaste 'fights' cavities. Even paper handkerchiefs, frailest and most disposable of articles, crackle with mettlesome aggression. Thus Scotties facial tissues are enlisted as a 'powerful partner' in the 'constant fight' against colds, allergies and sneezes. This militaristic rage is directed against enemies which are immaterial or sloppily liquid. Arid roll-on deodorant vows to 'fight odour and wetness'. Smells become solid objects, substances which the deodorant effortlessly pulverises. Behind these fantasies of bellicose cleansing prances the figure of the chivalric white knight, conducting his crusade on the soap-flake packets, and his ideology of armed sanctity routing the ugly evils of the world invades a product as innocuous as a powdery carpet cleaner: Plush brags that its powder is 'tough enough for stains too'. The chemical collision of cocky powder and arrogant stain is imaged as a wrestling match. The same admiration for products which surgically or therapeutically cauterise the shame of dirt has promoted 'lemony' to adjectival eminence in the detergent ads. Joy, for instance, is alleged to have a clean and lemony smell. Why invoke this sourest and most disdainful of fruits? Because lemons are acidulous, and acid like ammonia is thought to be efficient because brutally corrosive: like the puritan warrior on the white steed, it wields a sword with which it slices through corruption.

The greasy puddles and noxious spills with which the ads terrorise us are discharges of the guilt which persecutes the characters in the serials. A sinister ad for Comet casts the home-maker as the befouler. The salesman in the ad dares a housewife to concoct a stain which his product can't remove. She vows to 'make a mess you can't clean up', and sets about it with fiendish inventiveness, first smearing her kitchen sink with beets, then pouring over that a flask of dark rancid tea, afterwards rubbing in a blend of grease and pot-char. It's a grisly parody of cooking, as well as the evil obverse of cleaning, a little drama of transgression in which she vengefully besmirches the area which it's her marital duty to keep pristine. The salesman is tempting her to disgrace herself, because he wants to dramatise the distance between her fallible humanity and his abrasively pure, censorious product, which amazes the housewife by slicing through the murk with which she has muddied her sink. Ads like this enact a chemical penance, which corresponds to the psychotherapy patiently undergone by the soap characters. First our physical shame is blushfully aroused. Nancy Walker as Rosie the waitress in the Bounty paper-towel commercials classifies her customers according to the mess they make on her counter, like a crusty, judicial deity assessing our sinfulness. Everyone who enters her diner is a potential spill. Shame begets guilt, as if physical ordure or decay – the bad breath or whiffy wetness or lank hair about which the ads scold us – were the symptoms of moral weakness. Having incited our self-disgust, the ads then allay it by selling an instant remedy. Ad characters are made to suffer shame and guilt about the food they serve as well as about their bodies. 'My coffee's not so good,' moans a demoralised housewife. Her husband, with a weary grimace, agrees that it doesn't measure up to her cakes. She's distraught. Then she changes to mountain-grown Folger's, and all is well. The commercial's brevity makes the transformation magically instantaneous: happiness is attainable at once, if you purchase the approved brand.

Every article sold on the soaps contains within it the promise of perfection, of paradise restored. A floor-cleaner called Spic-and-Span is said to be 'barefoot clean'. The ad explains that Americans love to go barefoot (as if still in Eden), and Spic-and-Span ensures a floor worthy of their unshod soles. Cleanliness is no longer a bland absence of dirt. Its elevation to a spiritual and psychiatric virtue is signalled by the up-grading of 'clean' from a dependent adjective to a self-sufficient noun, in slogans like 'the *Gain* clean', and its endowment with sensory properties – 'a clean you can see, a fresh you can smell'. There is always a logic to television's arbitrary juxtapositions. Recovering innocence, venturing even to quicken the dead (Coast soap is credited with regenerative powers:

used in your morning shower, it's 'the eye-opener – it actually brings you back to life'), these ads recall the gloomy soap characters from their distresses and prescribe for them the cure which television itself has devised for our woes – the contentment of consumerism.

6
Games

Soap operas ingest the form of television and regurgitate it as content. The soaps could only exist on television because they're secretly about the conditions of that medium – its reduction of the viewer to morbid helplessness, its use as an occupier of vacant time, the consolation of its monotony and (in the ads) its prescription of a sudsy victory over despair. Game shows are another of television's self-celebrating inventions. The games are incitements to that romance of consumerism which is television's blissful dream, for they transform wealth from the product of our toil into a glibly instant conjuration of our wishes. They also attest to television's power as a broker of celebrity: hopeful nonentities are plucked from the barracking ranks of the studio audience, loaded with riches, then returned to their original oblivion. And at their most opulently technological, they actualise, like the plan in the 1950s for the *Today Show* studio, that glossy gadget-propelled future of which the television set itself is a premonition – a world of computerised score-boards, flashing lights and peremptory bleeps, in which people will have turned (as the game show hosts with their cloned blandness already have) into acquisitive robots.

The game shows evolved from the old radio quizzes, but in

the process the new medium altered the format to suit television's own idiosyncratic requirements. The early quizzes were jokey intellectual trials, superintended by pedagogic hosts called Professor Quiz or Dr I.Q. The quiz kids were miniature academics, capped and gowned, whose alacrity in answering the questions put to them was meant to urge their contemporaries to study harder at school. Information – the possession of answers to an infinity of possible questions, the capacity to spell all the most recondite words in the language – was the formula for success. The jackpots of the first television quizzes were rewards for mental skill. A radio show called *Take It or Leave It* had offered a $64 prize for a correct answer to one of its questions. Television multiplied the bonus a thousandfold and in 1955 introduced *The $64,000 Question*. This dizzying inflation of the spoils was accompanied by a new demand of encyclopaedic learning from the contestant. Only a polymath had a chance of winning. Here television began to have reservations about the form it had inherited from radio. Bergen Evans, who once prepared questions for *The $64,000 Question*, claimed that 'viewers don't like experts; they're too elitist.' Television was hostile to the suspense radio could extract from silence: those premonitory pauses during which the contestant struggled for the answer and risked losing all he'd won. Even a British quiz like *Mastermind* – which remains true to the intelligence test long since debauched by the American shows, and which with its leather chair and austere, inquisitorial spotlight rebukes the gimmicky gadgetry of its American counterparts – slights the expert by making him a specialised crank, who carries a world of otiose learning inside his head. *Mastermind*'s contestants, as well as answering general knowledge questions, nominate a special subject on which they are grilled. The narrower the field, the more donnishly minute must be their learning. Some contestants select the life and works of a single author or composer; others a war to which they're particularly partial; others a personal expanse of history or geography. Erudition like this, operating through the wrong end of the telescope, is perfectly adapted to television's own mode of miniaturisation. The small screen crowded with its millions of multicoloured specks is the size of a human head populated by meticulously accurate but irrelevant facts. Television emphasises (as in *Mastermind*) the cranky solipsism of scholarship, or (in America, where quiz question suppliers have gone on to compile anthologies of famous – meaning useless – first facts) its triviality.

Television can tolerate the expert only if he stages the agony of intellection as a performance. This was the venial crime of the quiz cheat Charles van Doren. He is one of television's martyrs. His sacrifice was demanded by the medium, because his faking was an offence against the spontaneity it claimed to prize. Though the exposure of van Doren changed the game shows – altering them from tests of mental aptitude to gambling ventures in which chance and luck and bluff count more than skill – he is the unacknowledged model for the programmes which followed his disgrace. Van Doren began his career on the quiz show *Twenty-One* in 1957 and accumulated $129,000 in prize money before being defeated. With an inspired charlatanism, he adapted the radio routine of question and answer to television by performing his replies. Sequestered in a sound-proof booth, he sweated and stuttered in a torment of frustration before finally delivering himself of the correct response. He had of course been coached in these antics, instructed in how to prolong the fidgety uncertainty, even supplied in advance with some of the answers he banged his brow to force out of hiding. Another contestant claimed in disgruntlement that he'd been bribed to lose to van Doren. The frauds were investigated by a grand jury and eventually by a committee of Congress, which subpoenaed van Doren. He admitted he'd been acting, and was denounced by President Eisenhower, who called the deception 'a terrible thing to do to the American public'. As a result of the investigation the shows were subjected to new legal restrictions, and in self-defence concentrated on styles of competition which couldn't be counterfeited; van Doren meanwhile put his expertise to work for the *Encyclopaedia Britannica*.

Now that the epidemic of moral indignation has abated, it's clear that the much-maligned riggers were actually pioneers. Though the medium reviled them, they were doing its work, turning the quiz from an aural examination into a visual spectacle, training contestants to be actors. Van Doren's opponent Herbert Stempel alleged that he'd been told to shear off his hair and wear a dilapidated suit. By looking impoverished, he was assured, he'd ingratiate himself with the audience. Was this a malpractice, or was it merely the medium's early, astute recognition that whatever happens on it must be a performance, and therefore a simulation? Even the leaking of answers had its apologetic aptness: nothing could illustrate better the medium's consumption of or its contempt for the messages it supposedly exists to transmit, since on television the questions are only a pretext for our spying on the contestants, and the answers are of interest not in themselves but only for the strain the contestant exhibits or affects as he arrives at them. To vindicate van Doren and the contest-fixers, the later game shows have taken to parodying the questions they ask. Here the pioneer was Groucho Marx, whose show *You Bet Your Life* guyed its contestants with queries like 'who's buried in Grant's tomb?' Groucho's act, like van Doren's mimicry of anguish in the isolation booth, was purely televisual. He asked the questions not to elicit answers but to gain time for us to relish the discomfiture of the victims he was twitting.

The format of question and answer suited radio because it's a ritualisation of that entirely aural art, conversation, the means by which we test, probe and decipher other people by more or less amiably interrogating them. Television has no patience with this inductive game of trial and error. Rather than inquisitively investigating people, it wants to observe and expose them. The questioner proceeds deferentially and diplomatically, finding out first one thing and then another, piecing together information. Television at once tired of such preliminaries, and has preferred to catch people unawares, to surprise them into self-revelation with its intrusively candid camera. Hence Groucho's demand that contestants tell him their most embarrassing moment. Television's speciality is such compulsory intimacies. For similar reasons, the sound-proof chambers to which contestants were relegated had no ventilation: sweat like ersatz make-up promoted the competitor to a performer by suggesting nervous panic. It's only fun to watch people answering questions if in doing so they admit us to some private recess of physical shame (as in the embarrassments exploited by Groucho) or mental turmoil (as in van Doren's desperate grimaces). Though television hounded van Doren into disgrace, all he'd done was to collaborate, by charmed instinct, with the medium.

So inimical is television to the expert and its confident answering of questions that it either subverts the quiz format or puts it into reverse. Merv Griffin devised a show called *Jeopardy* in which the contestants were supplied with the answers and then had to guess the questions. For instance, the question belonging to the answer '5,280' was 'How many feet are there in a mile?' The only knowledge television is interested in gauging is, like this, information which is self-evident or fatuous. *Hollywood Squares* not only chooses to ask ludicrously pseudo-scientific questions like 'Can you get a butterfly drunk?' or 'Is it true that surgery is most hygienically performed by women in the nude?', but hires a panel of comedians to answer on behalf of the contestants. The more inane and improbable the responses are, the better they're appreciated. Playing the game now means getting the answer inventively wrong. Other shows have settled on formulae which ask questions in order to bare the motives and assumptions of the answerers. *Card Sharks* tests not knowledge but consensus. It polls its audience on prurient or nonsensical subjects and determines an average opinion. Contestants on the show are tortuously required not to give their own answers to the questions but to guess the results of the poll. Specimen questions are 'Of 100 feminists how many have burned their bras?' or 'Of 100 female senior citizens how many have turned down a man for a second date because he got fresh on the first?' or 'Of 100 third-grade girls how many have tasted a mud pie?' One contestant guesses the poll percentage, while the other has to say whether the truth is higher or lower than that. The game cleverly begs the question of the answer, because its impertinent interest lies in exposing the contestants by interpreting their guesses. A ribald grannie for instance, in guessing a low percentage when asked the second of the above questions, reasons that the number must be small because in her own case she vetoes men if they fail to get fresh on the first date. Asked 'Of 100 Playboy bunnies how many would want to belong to a club where men waiters dressed in revealing costumes as jack rabbits?', an old biddy censoriously avows that few would, while a less prim younger woman guesses 70. The programme requires confidences from its viewers as well as from the game-players. On a recent episode the producers asked to hear from women who'd undergone breast-enlargement operations, so that a statistic for a future game could be calculated from their case-histories.

Increasingly the game shows ask questions not to obtain information or assess knowledge but to pillory people into self-exposure. Hence the lecherous probing of sexual habits on *The Dating Game* or *The Newlywed Game*. In *The Dating Game* three aspirant bachelors are secreted behind a partition from where they're quizzed by a nubile bachelorette, who has to decide from their replies which one she'll take on the date which is the show's prize. The men must sell themselves by their perky, pushful or huskily salacious responses, and are caught by the camera struggling, as all television's hapless subjects must, to confect a personality for themselves. The girl meanwhile proceeds with her humiliating inquisition. Among the things one recent bachelorette demanded to know about the men she was auditioning were 'What's the most degrading thing you ever made a girl do on a date?', 'What's the strangest thing you've ever taken to bed?', 'Which of your relatives corrupted you the most when you were a child and what was it they made you do?' and 'Where in public would you most like to undress?' *The Newlywed Game* likewise ransacks the soiled linen of a marriage. Husbands are asked what brand of underpants their wives will say they wear. This tests their proficiency as consumers at the same time as it robs them of their privacy. One spouse marked himself as a dolt by not knowing the brand of his own shorts. The host, assuming unfamiliarity with brand names to be proof of mental retardation, patiently explained that the brand was labelled at the back – if the man hadn't noticed the label, perhaps he couldn't tell his own back from his front. Some husbands and wives don't agree on the brand name of the disputed garment: thus the show can simultaneously convict them of ignorance as consumers and incompatibility as marriage partners. This scamy prying aims to provoke marital discord by showing how little each partner knows about the other. Wives, while their husbands are offstage, are asked to say what is their man's best feature. Husbands are then recalled and made to guess, with a maximum of lewd innuendo, which physical attribute their wives chose. Where the answers concur, there's giggly jubilation. But the programme's delight is to demonstrate disagreements, to sunder symbolically the freshly spliced pair.

Television's glory is the belittlement of people and the trivialisation of data, and the game shows are one of the medium's most playfully vicious institutions. Having abandoned the legitimate asking of questions, they not only parody their own original format but jovially denigrate their trusting contestants. Their treatment of the people who volunteer to play the games is an exact and nasty parody of television's recruitment and brusque dismissal of those on whom it confers celebrity. The medium's need for new faces makes it encourage everyone to believe himself a potential celebrity. Sooner or later the camera will alight on you, even if only as a passer-by in a newsreel of a traffic accident. I'm always surprised by the relaxed and unresentful willingness of people in the street to be interviewed by importunate newsteams. They hardly ever refuse, nor does their delivery falter. They know that their moment has finally come, and they calmly affront the challenge. Television has promised us that, in Warhol's phrase, everyone will sooner or later get to be world-famous – for fifteen minutes. An episode in Robert Young's situation comedy *Father Knows Best* was a fable about this televisual democratisation of celebrity. The family's elder daughter wins a competition seeking a lookalike for a singing film star, and is rewarded with a jaunt to Hollywood. There she is feted, and is so proud of being a famous person's double that she takes to impersonating the star, forging autographs for the fans who besiege her. When she's found out, she apologises to her father for her folly. He reassures her: to her friends and family she *is* a celebrity. Later, on a television interview, she asks permission to wish goodnight to the members of her fan club – her father, brother and sister, who are watching in the family home. They respond by saying goodnight to her image on the television screen. Movie stardom, the programme implies, is all self-falsification and existential imposture. On television you can become a star without ceasing to be your anonymous self, because the medium celebrates innocuous, domestic normality. Once on *The Tonight Show* Jack Paar maddened the studio audience by attentively quizzing one of its number and ignoring Cary Grant, who'd been planted in the adjoining seat. As well as a practical joke, this was a boast of television's licence to bestow celebrity on those it promiscuously or fortuitously favours. But the medium can just as easily rescind that celebrity. Obsolescence is built into the television star, as it is into the sets themselves: hence those mournful commercials for American Express in which the celebrities of yesteryear – the man who lent his croaky voice to Bugs Bunny, or a candidate for the Vice-Presidency in 1964 – laud the company's card, which restores to them an identity and a televisibility they'd forfeited.

The game show contestants experience this brief tenure of television celebrity – Warhol's fifteen minutes – at its most accelerated. But in order to qualify for it, they have to surrender themselves to the medium. Their only way of winning games is to abase themselves – feigning hysteria on *The Price is Right*, exchanging sordid confidences on *The Newlywed Game*, incompetently acting out inane charades on Bruce Forsyth's *Generation Game*. The cruellest of the games is *The Gong Show*, where one's span of celebrity may not even extend to fifteen seconds. More or less untalented contestants sing, dance, juggle or fiddle until the inevitable gong sends them back to nonentity. For some, the gong supervenes immediately. They've been warned this will happen, and coached to disappear with dignity, but are expected to go through with their act all the same and suffer their condemnation. Even a few seconds of television fame is worth the price of one's self-esteem. The show pretends to be a talent quest, but is a smirking parody of that.

The hosts on the game shows are, for similar reasons, parodies of geniality. A host soothes his guests and smooths obstacles out of their way. But in homage to Groucho, the comperes subject their victims to a ritual humiliation, and their patter keeps the game-players throughout flinching and ill-at-ease. In Britain the hosts are music hall comedians, who treat the contestants as obliging butts. The braying Bruce Forsyth on *The Generation Game* had a camera trained on him in permanent close-up to catch those sideways grins with which he mocked the people who were telling him, for instance, about their most embarrassing moment. His successor, limp-wristed Larry Grayson, exploits his own self-parodying effeminacy to make male contestants squirm. Even the host's inefficiency is a weapon against the unfortunate guest. When Forsyth stumbled over a name on one of his cue cards or Grayson couldn't focus his spectacles on those same cards, the guest would be jeeringly blamed for possessing so unpronounceable or illegible a name. The American hosts are even more suavely devilish. Richard Dawson baptises newcomers to *Family Feud* by planting a kiss on their lips. These pecks excited a controversy early in the programme's history, but by now have been accepted as essential to Dawson's manner of sly ingratiation. He says in his own defence that the kiss is a simple gesture of affection. But, on the contrary, it's a promise he doesn't mean to keep. He's flattering people he's never seen before by greeting them as old friends; however, as soon as the game dictates, he'll erase them without compunction. Dawson's style of slithery lechery – he moves with a predatory, gliding grace, and speaks with dreamy slowness, as if becalmed in an ecstasy of titillation – has been extended by Bob Eubanks on *The Newlywed Game*, who plays the insinuating serpent cajoling his victims and creating mistrust between them. Maxene Fabe in her book on the game shows quotes a specimen of his manipulative patter: 'He doesn't pay attention to you after you make love? Well, what *does* he do? And you put up with him, do you? Well, let's get him back out here and see what he has to say about that! Don't tell him? Why not? You just told *me*.' The concluding rebuke is especially ingenious. Eubanks has succeeded in getting a wife to tell him things she won't tell her husband, but he uses the information he's enticed from her both against the man and also (because to keep this new marriage going she has to be less than honest) against her. He's a voyeur posing as a confessor posing as a friendly therapist.

Hosts on the shows which distribute economic rewards rather than trafficking in connubial secrets have devised their own methods of initiatic guest-debasement. Ralph Edwards on *Truth and Consequences* prankily terrorised the studio audience. During warm-up sessions, someone pretending to be an audience member would be gunned down by Edwards's staff, as an example to the rest to stay in their seats; or a bandaged, stretcher-borne staff member would be displayed as one of yesterday's discarded contestants. Dawson and Eubanks trick their victims by offering an intimacy which they later withdraw; Monty Hall on *Let's Make a Deal* and Geoff Edwards on *The New Treasure Hunt* tantalise and torment their victims by appealing to their rapacity and playing on their self-doubt. To make a deal with Hall, you must first make a fool of yourself, caparisoning yourself as a cow or a playing-card or a soap-flake packet and seating yourself in a corral reserved for would-be contestants. If you're suitably laugh-able, he'll deign to notice you. Thereafter, you're at his mercy. The style of erotic confidentiality repellently perfected by Eubanks becomes in his case a cool confidence trickery, as he barters with his customers, using wallets, boxes and curtained showcases containing perhaps bonuses or perhaps booby-prizes. His purpose is to tempt the competitors to acts of improvidence. Playing the game means not costively retaining your winnings but risking them in return for what's lurking behind the curtain or in the box. The show's nastiest jest is to weigh down a contestant with unexpected wealth and then, because he or she has been encouraged by Hall to make another suicidal leap of faith, take all that money away: it's a small parable of television's bequest of celebrity, which is then abruptly and unpityingly cancelled. Some contestants, aggran-dised and enriched only to be deflated and impoverished all over again, refer to their career on the programme as if it were a speeded-up journey from life to death. They brought nothing onto the show, they reason, and will probably take nothing away from it. Given the meaninglessness of it all, why not act gratuitously? Monty Hall's infernal art is to inculcate in them this ludic recklessness. Similarly, on his treasure hunt, Edwards's role is that of devil's advocate. He's an imp of denial, who first wheedles a contestant into choosing a box and then marshals all his chattering power of persuasion to enforce betrayal of that choice by offering safer alternatives.

Persuading contestants to act imprudently, the hosts are converting them to the values of consumerism. The game shows as much as the soap operas are pretexts for commercials. The miseries of the soap operas are laved by the scourers and detergents marketed in the breaks, and the game shows are a training in the consumerism which the ads idealise. The games played on *The Price is Right* test the housewife's memory of what groceries cost. Behind them lies an evolution from a capitalist ethic of industry and thrift to a consumer capitalism fuelled by greedy fantasy. On the game shows you no longer need to labour to get rich: luck and the wilful ferocity of your wish (measured in the jubilant frenzy of the housewives chosen to compete on *The Price is Right*) will make you so. On both the games and the soaps, money is an adjunct of the exorbitant American romantic imagination. The soap people have to be affluent, so they can devote themselves full-time to the delectation of their private agonies. The game show people crave affluence, because for them it's a prerequisite of the celebrity with which television has temporarily blessed them. An early game called *Queen for a Day* recruited penurious women and made their acquisitive dreams come true. Each day the suppliants watched a procession of models exhibiting to them all the goods it was possible for them to win. Then one of the needy was chosen by the audience's vote. The electoral instrument was the applause meter: desert was equated with popularity, just as desire and fantasy had been equated with an unappeased longing for material luxuries. We all have the same serendipitous chance of wealth and celebrity in the consumer's heaven, because television makes its choices with inspiriting arbitrariness. The games are played without competitive rancour. No one envies another's good fortune because all of us share the same dreams and the same chance of having our wishes granted by television.

Stardom too is awarded by television with democratic impartiality. You don't have to be talented, and sooner or later we'll all have our turn. Hence those gleeful waves from the ranks when the cameras survey the studio audience at game show tapings. Being democratic, televisual celebrity is contagious. You can be famous by obliquity or association, and *Who Pays?* taunted the members of its panel by having them interview a celebrity's employees in an effort to guess the employer's identity. You can also be famous by resemblance or impersonation. *To Tell the Truth* lined up a real psychiatrist or diplomat or cleric with a pair of lookalikes and primed the imposters to bluff a panel of interrogators. Eventually the real psychiatrist or diplomat or cleric would be called on to stand up and declare himself. The bluffers were rewarded for successfully counterfeiting their own identity: for each mistake they lured the panel into making, they received a pay-off. During the long career of *To Tell the Truth*, the programme's scouts prowled the streets of New York spotting likely contestants. At any moment you might be stopped and asked to try out for the programme. Television had turned stardom into a cynosure of citizenship, a universal franchise. Consumerism aspires to distribute wealth in the same way: as the airlines put it, we want everyone to fly.

Canvassing the public to choose candidates for wealth and temporary fame, television institutes its own version of the census. The members of a studio audience are, without their knowing it, being surreptitiously screen-tested. *The Price is Right* claims to select its contestants randomly and spontaneously from the studio audience. In fact, it secretly auditions them while they're queueing outside before the programme begins. A staff member whose job it is to entertain those on the line first harangues them and then chatters with apparent inconsequentiality to each member of the crowd in turn. Everyone is name-tagged, and carries an admission ticket which is torn in half as the interviewer passes down the line. His catch-phrases as he gossips with one person after another send signals to his entourage. Hearing him enthuse in talking to people who are exceptionally eager or good-humoured or zany, his attendants note the names of the chosen ones, who once inside will be invited by Johnny Olson to 'Come on down!' Even if you don't qualify and remain stranded in the bleachers, you'll be required to donate to the show a compulsory hilarity. Professional barkers and flashing signs enjoin you to applaud; if your enjoyment is inadequate, it's mechanically boosted by a laughter track. All of us are television's unwitting conscripts.

The medium has devised a millennial future for us, of which the game shows are a prevision. The future is a consumer's paradise, and the game show studios are labs of gadgetry furnished with its hardware – an IBM sorter on *The $64,000 Question* to shuffle questions, a self-operating typewriter on *The $10,000 Big Surprise.* No longer testing meagre human intelligence, the games rely on the electronically efficient brain of the computer. Theirs is a world for cybernauts, and the games often appear to be engineering their bemused human participants into robotry. The hosts are a breed of plastic men, with teeth as perfect as chromium and hair the springy consistency of astroturf, and they look – as befits plastic – as if they could be infinitely duplicated. Their banter is a clockwork conviviality, for they're incapable of improvisation. Even Groucho in *You Bet Your Life* read his jests from an overhead screen. The relentless patter of the off-camera announcers sounds automated, like a record revolving too fast. This too is deliberate: because the networks strictly limit promotional puffs for merchandise given away on the show to eight seconds per item, the announcer has to train himself to race through the product's credentials before the stopwatch rules against him – hence the mechanical velocity of his utterance. Contestants are also uncannily metamorphosed. The women on *The Price is Right* bounce, squeak and gibber like wind-up toys manically out of control. Like human sacrifices in a scientific experiment, they're prisoners of technology. On the early quizzes they were often wired up like felons inside their sound-proof booths where, while they deliberated over their answers, they were ultrasonically assaulted with a high-pitched, nerve-shredding musical tone. Bells, buzzers and (on *The New Treasure Hunt*) resounding klunks admonish them. On *Family Feud* they're equipped with their own means of electronic murder: lock-out devices which, when pressed, sentence a slow-reflexed rival to silence.

As a comedy of consumerism, the game shows, like the soaps, are one of television's self-images. The set itself is a necessary luxury, and its presence in the home plugs us into the treasury of consumer durables which the ads hector us to buy and which the game shows distribute for free. Soon we'll be able to use our receivers for marketing as well as window-shopping. Subscribers to the Qube cable system in the United States can check comparative prices at local supermarkets on their set, and punch out orders on a console which relays their needs to the station and thence to the store. In the games, television celebrates the wealth which it both maximises and symbolises.

7
Ads

Expenditure is for most of us a grudging and self-wasting business, a dissipation of our resources. Commercial television proposes to change that by inciting us to buy things. Programmes are its decoys – packages for the articles on display in the ads. The game shows serve television's ideology of consumerism by turning expenditure into adventure. The customer is redefined as the player, the consumer who in disbursing his funds is not merely closing a transaction and acquiring something he can use but embarking on a career of self-augmentation and self-renovation. Everything we buy is these days appraised as something to be consumed, no matter whether we intend to eat it or wear it or ride in it or watch or listen to it. We consume our purchases because our aim in buying them is to absorb them into ourselves. Just as we masticate food into sustenance, so we're told that we ought to engorge the after-shave or pairs of jeans or brands of detergent or sleek new cars foisted on us by the ads and transmute them into feelings. It's feelings which the ads peddle – the thrill of aromatic or hip-hugging sensuality, the prim sanctity of cleanliness, the arrogance of ownership and technical mastery. Affluence has cured us of economic necessity. The things we're now assured we can't do without are always luxuries, super-fluities. Television's tactic is therefore first to instil an appetite and then minister to it. Products in the ads nowadays volunteer to do things to us, rather than merely – as in the drab utilitarian past – for us. No longer slavishly content to relieve us (which was technology's original promise to care-worn humanity), they want to remake us. Nothing will ever be the same, we're promised, after we drink Smirnoff vodka.

Our heady and intimidating responsibility as consumers is to live up to the ambitions which the things we buy conceive for us. A while ago in New York I bought a pair of shoes. The salesman refused to believe that I wanted them for any purpose so drearily terrestrial as walking. He enthused over the excellence as dancing pumps of the pair I'd chosen – their slinkiness, their springiness, their detachable inner soles for aeration after bouts of frenzied stomping. Having sold them to me, he ushered me out of the shop calling after me, 'Enjoy the shoes – you'll *love* them!' That's the litany of the new, messianic consumerism, which has even taken to using its prized verb 'enjoy' as an intransitive injunction. I was wrong to ask no more of my shoes than that they should be comfortable. Like that conspicuous consumer Gatsby with his wardrobe of shirts, I had a duty to enjoy them, to reward them with my love for the alteration they were bound to make in my life, for the choreographic resilience they were to bring to my tread. I'm still trying to be worthy of my shoes. I've realised remorsefully that the absence of enthusiasm as a consumer marks one as apathetic, maybe even mentally regressive. A television ad for bleach offers a grim and acne-pocked adolescent, his throat festooned with sharks' teeth, the chance of comparing his bleached small clothes with another pile laundered only in detergent. His mother apologises to the announcer in charge of the demonstration, saying that her son doesn't care. The teenager's own sullen comment is 'I'm not into wash.' In the country of consumers, to remain unmoved by the miracle of wash is – we're made to feel – as bad as being dirty.

Consumerism revises our relation with the things we own. It

transubstantiates possessions: material spoils become spiritual benefits. The erstwhile hero of capitalism was the miser, shrewdly hoarding what he had, gloating like Volpone over a wealth which for him had a cupidinous value in itself rather than as a means of exchange. The heroic figure of consumerism is not the accumulator of wealth but the big spender who has cast off the retentive inhibitions of the puritan conscience and converts wealth into instant gratifications. The housewives who wheel, deal, bluff and risk all on the game shows are the gleeful exponents of consumerism.

The game shows have outgrown the old economic world of aggressive acquisition, though sometimes they glance back at it. *Supermarket Sweep*, for instance, turned the lanes of the market into a turf on which housewives did battle, propelling trolleys as their chariots, with nimble outriders poised to grab at the merchandise. The woman crossing the finishing line at the check-out desk with the costliest shopping-cart of booty won the game and kept the goods she'd pillaged. One woman from Levittown, New York, managed in a few minutes to plunder thirty-five turkeys, twenty-two lawn chairs, a ton of meat and canned foods, and a trip to the Bahamas. Enrichment, according to this game, is scrambling warfare. *Money Maze* even more savagely reduced the process to a rat-race, a scuttling quest for provender. Here the supermarket was remodelled to resemble a behaviouristic catacomb, through which the competing housewives scampered in pursuit of prizes. Their husbands, overlooking the maze from a rostrum, egged them on and bellowed directions. *Supermarket Sweep* interpreted the struggle for commodities as an epic combat of clashing trolleys; *Money Maze* scaled it down to sordid, subterranean ferreting. But on both shows you had to grapple, bustle and exert yourself to stay alive. The new game shows proceed differently. The consumer no longer needs to be greedy and grasping. If you wish for the products hard enough and vow to love them and be loyal to them, they'll come to you.

Consumerism changes acquisition from a chariot race in the supermarket aisles into a lazy home-bound day dream, which television can bring to pass. On *The Price is Right* acquisition is an effortlessly wishful association of ideas. A contestant won a swimming pool, with a wishing well as a bonus. When she used the well to wish for a car, the show supplied her with one. The more extravagant jackpots on *The Price is Right* – tabulated in Maxene Fabe's book – purified wealth of its grossness, changing squalid lucre into otiose, ornamental, consumerist fantasy. Someone who won a colour television set was awarded as an extra a live peacock to help in adjusting the colour. Occasionally prizes were coupled with bonuses which contradicted them. The winner of a home soda fountain received in addition a fully-equipped gym, in which the family of gormandisers could work off the weight they'd put on at the fountain; the winner of some shares of railway stock got as a bonus a safe to keep them in, and a chihuahua to stand ineffectual guard over it. The deflatory coupling is deliberate, a reminder that the wealth the game shows disburse isn't vulgar material gain (the fatty soda fountain, the anal-erotic strongbox) but spiritual uplift, hedonistic joy. For the consumer it's chic to divest yourself of your wadding of wealth, to boast that you're unencumbered by it. Hence the gym with its slimming gear, and the chihuahua to deride the safe by pretending to squat on sentry duty outside it.

The market – in *Supermarket Sweep* or *Money Maze* an arena or a behavioural cage – alters its function on the new game shows. Acquisition is now an affair of dazing chance, and the studios with their fickle wheels and dicey bargaining resemble Las Vegas casinos. Acquisition has at the same time been refined into a game of skill, and the shows often revert to the pedantic drill of the classroom. Consumerism demands of its adepts an educated alertness and a gift for impromptu mental arithmetic. You have to be able to balance the claims of competing brands by calculating the ratio between quantity and cost. The consumer isn't just cravenly buying things: she's grading and assessing them or computing with them. The game shows test this expertise. The women on *The Price is Right* are often asked to assemble a basket of groceries which will total say between $6.75 and $7. They can win only if they've taught themselves to memorise supermarket prices. Yet this requirement of rote-learning, which treats consumerism as connoisseurship, is made in an atmosphere of languorous sensuality. *The Price is Right* retains a harem of slinky sales-girls who uncover the washing machines and stereo sets which are exhibited as prizes and prod the cash register with their crimson nails during the grocery games. Their presence serves to ally consumerism with concupiscence. The motive of capitalism used to be greed; consumerism has commuted that motive into sexual desire. Aiming as it does to make us crave things we don't need, to arouse appetites, consumerism's aptest way of succeeding is to make us randy. But the object of our stirrings isn't the models, it's the products they're commending. People on the television ads have carnal congress with their appliances. The man who announces in satiated tones 'Boy, did I get stroked this morning' is complimenting his razor. The woman who confesses 'I like to start my day with a couple of soft strokes' is referring to her roll-on deodorant.

As well as enticing us to lust for hardware instead of human bodies, consumerism boasts of its victory over economic necessity by striving to make us hungry when we don't need to eat. This is why television has so charmed a relation with the junk food it advertises. We watch television between meals, when we oughtn't to be thinking about food, but the medium exploits our suggestibility by encouraging us to slaver at the chocolate bars, potato crisps and popcorn it's selling. Consuming these unnutritious victuals isn't eating so much as the repletion of a bored and querulous vacancy, as indeed is watching television. One of the mixtures of toffee and chocolate advertised on British television presents as its chief virtue the time it takes to chew. Disconsolate queuers at a bus stop snap at their chocolate bars and gobble them up at once. The chap armed with the correct brand is still contentedly toiling over his when – presumably hours later – the bus arrives. This is a kind of eating which, like gaping at television, is a substitute for doing anything, a condition of inane passivity. The original technological revolution was about saving time, shortcutting labour; the consumerism which is the latest instalment of that revolution is about wasting the time we've saved, and the institution it deputes to serve that purpose is television. The ads are always admonishing us to stop working. A dishwasher volunteers to relieve us of our chores, saying 'Sit, America – we'll do the washing up.' But what do we do while we're not washing up? Television's answer is smugly self-referring: we watch television, and on it we see the dishwasher uncomplainingly toiling on our behalf.

The dishwasher's address to us typifies consumerism in being half ingratiation (the machine, an abject slavey, sacrifices itself to be of assistance to us) and half injunction (we're ordered to sit, enjoined not to interfere, as if our competence were being questioned). Are we the thing's owner or its admiring, incapable spectator? Consumerism likes to flatter us by pandering to our freedom of choice and obsequiously catering to our leisure, but all the time it's accomplishing the opposite – regimenting us, depriving us of our freedom, making us the complacent maws into which it shovels its products. We are all colleagues of the bewildered women on the game shows who, though made to believe they can deal and gamble their way to a fortune, are actually the victims of sly manipulation. Manufacturers are happy to lavish prizes on them, because in doing so they've secured free advertising. The women are goaded with the allurement of riches, but the only dreams the game shows can bring true are dreams which covet a stockpile of consumer durables.

The ad campaigns for junk food pretend that each of us is

the only customer in the world. The consumer is less customer than patron: he can insist that the product fit his requirements. Macdonalds and Burger King pharisaically claim that this is the logic of their operation. The hamburgers they sell are of course standardised, identical, therefore fast and reliable, the same everywhere, and in persuading us to eat them they're imposing a similar standardisation on us. (A British television ad for Bird's Eye beef burgers derives a sardonic comedy from this equation between the similitude of the products and that of the people who consume them. A girl, presiding over a supper being eaten by her younger brother, wonders where the boy's twin is, since his favourite burgers are getting cold. The boy rushes out, calls his twin, pretends to answer, hastily rearranges his dress and returns, impersonating the other, to gobble up the second burger – at which point the missing twin arrives, apologising for his lateness.) We're as disposable and dispensable as the plastic cutlery and paper napkins. Customers are processed through these fast food emporia as impersonally as the hamburgers, embarked on an unslumbering conveyor belt. But consumerism can't admit this. Macdonalds and Burger King, which have enriched themselves by treating us as if we were all the same, elaborately defer in their ads to the individual caprices and desiderata which are the whimsical life of consumerism. 'You, you're the one,' chants Macdonalds, 'we do it all for you,' and Burger King invites us to 'have it your way', which means fastidiously selecting whichever combination of lettuce, pickle, onion and mayonnaise you want smeared on your bun. But if you saunter into a Burger King concession intending to have it your way, you'll find that unless you're prepared to wait (which defeats the purpose of eating fast food) you'll have to join the express line, above which is posted the order 'have it *our* way'. Consumerism's fond fallacy is to pretend that mass production, rather than rendering all our needs uniform, serves the idiosyncratic expectations of each customer.

The assembly line thus changes from a deadening mechanical replication to an exercise in freaky, unrepeatable virtuosity. A recent British commercial made the point by taking two minutes to show Fiat Strada cars being assembled by robots to the accompaniment of a speeded-up, voiceless, electronically boosted version of Figaro's introductory aria from Rossini's *Il barbiere di Siviglia*. The musical choice had an inspired aptness. Rossini was celebrated for the almost technological facility of his composition, and stories were told about him scribbling an overture in the time it took for a pan of rice to come to the boil. He thus anticipates Fiat's nimble robots, and magics their cybernetic skill into dazzling art. As a result, although the commercial was four times as long as most, its paradoxical effect was to suggest abbreviation not prolongation – the bravura foreshortening of time by technology. Figaro himself is an apt patron saint for Fiat's new car. In that opening aria he brags of his ubiquity and his utility as a factotum for the whole city of Seville: he's as manoeuvrable, as adventurous and as speedy as the car. His aria also lightly converts technical difficulty into display, and implies that the robots are – like him – not mechanical genii but larky, ebullient show-offs. Standardisation, here as in the fast food commercials, adapts itself to consumerism by declaring that each of its indistinguishable products has an individual life and purpose. Macdonalds do it all for *you*; the Fiat robots become performers, who will never sing an aria the same way twice, and who are in the business not of constructing machines for us but, like opera singers, of entertaining us. So determined is consumerism to convince its client that he is the sole object of its fawning attentions that in a notorious series of National Airlines commercials stewardesses introduced themselves to the viewer and offered him, by alluring implication, not a seat on a plane but a rendezvous at the end of the journey: 'Hi, I'm Karen – fly me.'

Mechanical reproduction is fatal, as Walter Benjamin

pointed out, to the aura of people and of art-objects. In duplicating them it obliterates that halo of singleness and integrity which protects them. Television deprives people of their individuality, flattening and reducing them, and replaces the aura it has confiscated with the cheery mechanised gloss it calls personality or the rigged and phoney celebrity it calls stardom. The ads, ministering to a consumerism which insists that every product is a unique gift of grace and every customer a patron whose needs the product devotes itself to satisfying, preoccupy themselves with the application of aura to products which, manufactured in their millions, never possessed it. Products in the ads radiate an invincible aura which they owe entirely to the manufacturer's rhetoric: toothpastes, mouth wash, soap and deodorants armour you inside a shield of confident cleanliness, a sanitary cordon which is their enchanted aura. Aura alchemically converts products to potions. Sometimes the products destructively assert themselves, as an angry aura demolishes the packaging which cages it. A brand of lager, advertised as thirst-shattering, pulverises the brick of ice inside which it's penned. But the aura is the result either (as here) of hyperbole, or of simulation. Television, which erases the reality of human beings and puts in its place the slick uniform of stardom, makes even commercial products belie their own reality and play its game of dissimulation. The Cinzano Bianco in a current series of British ads is a concoction of water, lime juice and Coca Cola. A swig of Cinzano Rosso is added, but only to tone up the colour, not as a concession to authenticity.

Like the game shows, consumerism toys malevolently with those on whom it rains its favours, and the human beings who ally themselves with those bold, boastful products in the ads are subject to a subtle cheapening. Why are actors so superstitiously ashamed of doing television commercials? Because they know it will be their fate to be upstaged by the product they're sponsoring. The product's the performer, and the actor must consent to be its intimidated stooge. In agreeing to do the commercial, the actor is signing away his own aura, leasing it to the product, and collaborating in an often cruel though apparently inadvertent self-mockery. After his retirement as Metropolitan Police Commissioner for London, Robert Mark performed in a series of testimonials for a brand of automobile tyres. He defended himself by donating the money to charity, but people all the same were shocked, as if a policeman had been caught pocketing a bribe.

Even more ignominious than the taint of self-prostitution, is the imputation of self-parody. The television ad is the genre into which the superannuated actor declines, and in being assigned to a specific product he often finds himself pillorying his own past and apologising for his present distressed state. Margaret Hamilton, the Wicked Witch of the West from *The Wizard of Oz*, turns up in the ads as Cora, proprietrix of a country store. This wizened martinet, now deprived of the devilish powers she exploited in the movie, can only bossily require her customers to buy Maxwell House coffee. Lorne Greene of *Bonanza*, put out to pasture, these days makes ads for puppy food. The epic rancher dwindles to a breeder of tame pet dogs; the patriarch of the Ponderosa, whose three sons have outgrown him, has only his litters of dogs to care for, and instead of familial education (the homiletic burden of the *Bonanza* episodes) he's concerned with canine nutrition. Robert Young, who played the genial physician Marcus Welby, currently lends his para-medical authority to Sanka decaffeinated coffee. Here the conjunction between actor and product diminishes the former while legitimising the latter. The family doctor is now occupied with curing himself: caffeine agitates his nerves, and Sanka enables him to enjoy his addiction without suffering the consequences. Bereft of the communal prestige he possessed on the series, he's passed it on, in his retirement, to the product: Sanka, promoted by him, becomes a doctor's prescription. Perhaps the most piquant case of the ad as a symbol of the actor's superannuation is the announcements Frank Borman has made for Eastern Airlines. Grounded, the astronaut extols the superiority of an airline in which other men do the flying. His own function is to make propaganda for his company's efficiency in that most earth-bound of departments, baggage handling. Occasionally the ads supply the obsolete performer with a covert self-vindication. In 1980 Bert Parks was retired as compere of the Miss America Pageant. At 65, he was considered too old. Parks promptly made an ad for a brand of coffee which parodied the pageant from which he'd been excluded: a coffee tin, sprouting svelte female legs, parades on the catwalk while Parks proudly officiates. The banishment of Parks to the ads is a sneaky comment on the pageant itself, which plasticises and packages the contestants as if they were synthetic concoctions, and merchandises them like the coffee tins which are the new objects of Parks's serenade.

The ads often demote or demobilise their characters, ejecting them from television's fictions and stranding them in a drab modern world. Hudson (Gordon Jackson), the punctilious butler from *Upstairs, Downstairs*, has had to accept the vulgar novelty of the supermarket, and can be seen half-heartedly hymning the produce which clutters the aisles of Fine Fare. Or else the ads enfeeble characters who seemed hitherto unassailably heroic. Don Meredith, the rugged jock, turns up advertising not whisky or some other locker-room libation but Lipton's tea. Despite this evidence of commercial shame and self-diminution, some people choose the television ad as a genre to excel in, because they see it as a vehicle of that pure, contentless celebrity which only television can award. Fame used to be a reward for something you had done. Television however deals not in self-ennobling achievement but in gossipy hearsay and glossy immediacy: it has no sense of the past, so how can it commemorate a life's history of ambitions and victories? For television, what you've done is as defunct as yesterday's news. The past is only recycled when you die, and the news department resurrects ancient film-clips. To replace fame, television has its own mode of enshrinement, which is celebrity. On television you become a celebrity by being visible, just as in the gossip columns you become one by being talked about. The charm of this sanctification is easy to understand – it means being loved for your meagre self, not for any qualities which might mitigate that self, and it's therefore everyone's dream. As a result, people who can pride themselves on individual gifts, and who might therefore be content with mere fame, hanker after celebrity as well, because they know it has nothing to do with acclaim for their artistry and is a matter simply of recognition not approbation. This is why Luciano Pavarotti or Orson Welles do television ads. Pavarotti's appearances on behalf of American Express confide his lovable, deplorable longing to be famous not just for being a great singer, but – with luminous self-sufficiency – for being famous. Or even for being fat: he also, between operatic performances, cooks spaghetti on talk shows. Welles, too, in his lager or sherry commercials capitalises on his *embonpoint*. The celebrity after all is someone whose face or body you remember, not someone whose talents you admire. In the lager series, Welles enjoys the ultimate condition of celebrity, imposing himself while remaining invisible. His voice alone is used, but it's fat and fruity enough to evoke the body from which it resonates.

Though the ads enrich those who appear in them, they exact their own penalty. They're an extreme case of that trivialisation to which television subjects all its human agents: people here sacrifice themselves to products, squander their reputations in the service of dog chow and coffee-less coffee. Jonathan Price in his book on the ads, *The Best Thing on TV*, finds in them a buried but violent resentment which surfaces in assaults on the accident-prone products. He charts the vicissitudes of a few manufacturers' samples. Suitcases are tossed, mauled, gored, and stamped on by a football team, or hurled onto the highway from a fast car. An insurance company demolishes a house, and Minolta detonates a camera. A screen of polyethylene film is battered by a rabid bull, a security padlock is bombarded with bullets. Cars are dropped from aeroplanes or driven over waterfalls. Even in the supermarket, the wares are subjected to impudent indignities: hence Mr Whipple's vigilant prohibition of Charmin-squeezing. Jonathan Price interprets these consumer disasters as expressions of a stifled rage against the products which bully us into buying them. If he is right, then the ads which prop up capitalism are secretly inciting us to revolutionary aggression. But I don't believe he is right, for what his catalogue of examples proves is precisely the indestructibility – and, in the case of Mr Whipple's enticingly soft Charmin toilet tissue, the inviolability – of products. In another of the ads, a parachutist loses his Timex watch at a height of 800 feet. It plummets to earth, and when found is still valiantly ticking. It's not the products which are being put at risk, but their human users. Consumerism views its customers as a necessary inconvenience. We're necessary because we have to buy the products, but once we own them we manhandle and mistreat them, hurling watches through the air, denting suitcases, crashing cars. The private yearning of consumerism is for a world in which its products will no longer be the victims of incompetent humans, in which people will have been dispensed with. A brand of British motor oil is making ready for this robotised future, since its television ads present it as the oil 'which protects the car against the human race'. The ads are not, as Price believes, our vendetta against the supercilious products. They record the opposite war, of the products against their temporary human legatees. They are consumerism's boast that the things it makes are too good for the inept and messy humans on whom they're lavished. *Mary Hartman, Mary Hartman* was about the fatality of consumerism. Here the products, insufficiently cherished by those who should have loved and propitiated them, as I was instructed to do with my new shoes, fought back – characters choked on television dinners, were drowned in vats of chicken soup, or electrocuted by television wires in the bath water. Mary, cautioned by these executions, spends her days earning the respect of her products and perfecting her skills as a consumer. She's traumatised by her failure at brewing coffee. 'What am I going to do about my coffee?' she worries. 'I've tried *every* kind of coffee – perc, drip.' She and her husband Tom have a reverent trust in brand names. Tom drinks a can of Schlitz before dinner, and will tolerate no other kind of beer; Mary when confronted by a family crisis invokes a brand name as if superstitiously crossing herself: 'I should have fixed pancakes – Hungry Jack's extra-thin pancakes.' Those talismanic slogans, because they belong so intimately to the characters, also have a tincture of erotic suggestiveness to them. 'Can you tell me where the nearest House of Pancakes is?' inquires Mary seductively of the policeman she fancies. The joke of the series was that the people on it behaved exactly like their counterparts on the television commercials, and in their world a consumer mishap has all the grisly excitement of a traffic accident: Grandpa, debating whether to spend the day in the park playing checkers or at Safeway watching them unload melons, chooses the latter option, remarking with murderous glee, 'Sometimes they drop one.'

Most of the time consumerism is engaged in persuading us to buy things we can do without, in redefining luxury as necessity. The ads, dramatising the persuasion, therefore emphasise the spiritual or psychic bounty with which the product will bless us. Products are anthropomorphised, and their human purchasers turn into their abject beneficiaries, whose self-esteem is enhanced by the things they own. Commercial transactions become existential transfers, enlivening the manufactured product and magicking it into a process, a formula for the happiness of its owner. The purpose of the ads is to fictionalise the things they're promoting. Even perhaps to mythologise them – which means to ally them with the gods who prompt and reprove us. Advertising is a mythopoeic activity, because its surest way of coaxing us into buying is to resurrect those parental deities whose power we still slavishly acknowledge. It makes credulous infants of us all over again, and subjects us to the tyranny of demiurges like the chuckling Green Giant, cosy Aunt Jemima, the broodingly virile Marlboro Man, or that intercessor who frees us from the consequences of our fleshly appetites, Speedy Alka-Seltzer. The age of advertising is a latter-day age of faith, which reconstitutes myths and ritualises the dreary secular routine of our existence. Ruskin constrasted the godless nineteenth century's notion of morning as a sleepy, reluctant 'return to frivolous amusement, or fruitless labour', with the Greek invention of Apollo driving his chariot, who charges sunrise with symbolic meanings – 'daily restoration to the sense of passionate gladness, and of perfect life, . . . the thrilling of new strength through every nerve'. The sun correspondingly changes from an importunate alarm clock to 'a spiritual power'. The ads have assumed this duty to rehabilitate moribund myths, restoring the sense of rite and worship to our reawakening. Showers become baptisms; soaps precious life-givers; breakfast a libation of liquid sunshine (if we drink Florida orange juice) or an access of burgeoning, bouncy vitality (if we chew on those vitamin elves who snap, crackle and pop in the cereal bowls) or a benign family communion (if Thomas's English muffins are served instead of toast).

Myths are unriddlings of our own perdition. They explain to us why we were ejected from paradise, and consolingly show us the way back there. In each individual life that collective expulsion from happiness is replicated when we outgrow our childhood. It's therefore infancy with its unreflecting joy which the ads promise to restore. No food ever tastes so good as that on which we gorge when we're young. The food ads consequently market memories of those antediluvian meals. Biscuits, sealed as tightly as time-capsules, are labelled with the assurance that 'Pepperidge Farm remembers', and Breyer's ice-cream is accompanied by a pledge of purity and a testimony that it has been all-natural since 1866 – in America a virtually pre-historic, mythological date. The food ads are set in a pastoral idyll where the biscuit-making factory is a nostalgic farm, where grandmother ground her coffee beans with grain to rid them of bitterness, and where the menopausal Mouseketeer Annette Funicello convinces families camping beside a lake of the nutritional value of Skippy peanut-butter sandwiches. (One of Annette Funicello's erstwhile colleagues, Charles Laney, has traded in his ears for a career in consumerism, and regards his period on *The Mickey Mouse Club* as the best possible vocational training: he now manages a supermarket in San Diego, where he sees it as his responsibility to perform for his customers as well as selling to them – 'my customers know who I am and they expect me to keep them entertained, and I love to do it!')

But sadness betrays the idyll. We all know that the happy garden with its camping holidays and peanut-butter sandwiches is irrecoverable. While busying themselves with feeding us, the ads are offering to appease a more unassuageable hunger, and failing to do so. The food won't be equal to our expectations or fond memories. The product is certain to disappoint, but the ad, wistfully reconciling us to our loss by enabling us briefly to revisit the desecrated pastoral, won't: the ad is its own justification. Because consumerism is – in the case of food – marketing sentiments rather than tastes, the products seem to exist in order to occasion the ads which are their poetic apotheoses. The Pepperidge Farm package with its rusticated lettering and its intact, foil-guarded central safe has a symbolic value to which the biscuits it contains are secondary and maybe superfluous.

Ads

The ads have other fables about adulthood. One compensation for the disillusionment of growing up is that we get to own a car. Acquiring a driver's licence is, in America, the adolescent's formal graduation to maturity. As a result, while the food ads recall us to a pastoral state of infantile dependence and simplicity, the ads for cars – another of television's home-grown genres – urge us ahead into aggressive, epic adulthood. The machines are personified as specimens of masculine dominance: Toronado cars are 'broad-shouldered, massively male'. And in contrast with the bucolic settings bespread with Annette Funicello's peanut butter, the landscapes favoured for the car ads are sited further west, in the austere, eroded spaces defied by the epic American pioneers: automobiles perch in places which are implausible or impossible but, given the mythology of advertising, poetically true, on the edge of the crater at the Grand Canyon or atop the pinnacles of Monument Valley. Cars westernise their urban owners. The ads – computing horsepower and fondling the leather upholstery as if the seat were a saddle, associating the machines with the untameable predators of epic landscape like the Buick eagle, caging a tiger in the petrol tank – make the driver a combatant, a man who, bestriding his engine and aphrodisiacally revving it, is armed against the challenges and enmities of grown-up life. All this is of course a fiction. In life no one can afford to use a car as an instrument of will, battering obstacles into submission. The driver has to be a timid law-abider or else he'll lose his licence, and these days there are restrictions on speed to prevent him from enjoying the exhilarating capacities of his machine. But this doesn't deter the ads, for it's precisely their function to improve on the deflating actuality. Once again they're truer than the truth. They exult in the bellicose symbolic meaning of owning and driving a car, even though that symbolic possibility has been censured and belittled by reality. The competitive chariot-racing thrills which have been outlawed on our faint-hearted highways can now be had solely by watching the ads. There too you'll see cars being subjected to extremes of stress and shock which ordinarily they'd avoid – driven over endurance courses, plummeting over waterfalls, somersaulting down rocky hills, even dumped from a plane. No one who owned a car would do these suicidal things to it, but one of the machine's symbolic meanings is its aptitude for this kind of self-tormenting trial. It suffers on the driver's behalf, and its mechanical indifference to obstacles serves to make a man of him. It's at once the urban cowboy's mount and his weapon. But not any more on the roads – only in the enchanted mythic province of the ads, which here make good another of our impoverishments.

Both the food and car ads are unavailing fantasies. The ads specialising in deodorants and detergents more realistically purvey relief from the present torment of anxiety. Sweat, euphemised by the ads as wetness, is a gross fault because it's the exterior admission of inner turmoil. The ads always re-present it as an affliction visited on harried businessmen, as if it were the exhalation of their ugly doings throughout the day. In the mercantile city where these ads are set, virtue is equated with dryness, business ethics with corporeal probity. Back in the suburbs the wives of these hygienically desiccated execu-tives can be found in other ads scouring and bleaching in their laundries, militantly deodorising their rugs, degreasing their hair with medicated shampoo, and pausing to steady them-selves with decaffeinated drinks which won't agitate their already frayed nerves. Like their husbands at the office, the women in their battle against smells and stains are expung-ing guilt. But what's the source of this guilt? In deodorised America, it's the puritan disdain of self-disgust; in scruffier Britain it's less a prim recoil from the squalor of the body than an exclusively social shame. Snobbery is the British equivalent to the American conviction of spiritual unworthiness. In America you have to supplicate to your products and promise to be grateful to them for the dirty work you've made them do in cleansing your house and your body; in Britain you have to ensure that you're socially (not spiritually) worthy of your products. A current ad makes a parable from this British fear of being socially humiliated by one's disdainful possessions. A husband and wife return home to find the house bare. Their furniture (a note explains) has fled because it can't bear to live with their nasty gas fire. Mortified, they hasten to invest in a new fire and their furniture, relenting, rejoins them. As they bask in the gaseous glow, a vinyl armchair slides forward of its own accord, nudging its deferential owners aside as it warms itself. The couple congratulate each other on having at last earned the social esteem of their living-room suite. They're now on visiting terms with their furniture. Consumerism is forever taunting us in this way with our failure to merit its benediction. Just as the actors in the ads find themselves demeaned and derided by the products they're so conscientiously flattering, so all of us are reproved by our upstart appliances – all we do is soil or exhaust them, enslaving them to our chores or (in the case of those deodorants, tampons and rolls of bathroom tissue) obnoxiously acquainting them with our less savoury physical processes. Technology secretly dreams of dispensing with the human nuisances whose lives it supposedly exists to aid. A television commercial for a telephone-answering machine has Alexander Graham Bell lament that there's only one thing his invention won't do: answer itself. Supplied with the answering device, he thanks the manufacturers, declaring, 'Now it's perfect.' He means perfectly self-sufficient, since it can now entertain itself and need no longer trifle with the clumsy human users who break into its solipsistic circuitry.

Television has lent itself so patiently to the uses of consumerism because the set itself is a trophy of consumerism – its presence in the house enrols us as members of the affluent society – as well as a theatre for the cavorting of consumer durables on the game shows or in the ads. Watching television, we're dually consumers, of the medium (as spectators) and of the goods it's displaying (as potential customers). The screen is a shop window, the box a warehouse. Inside it, everything is packaged and price-tagged. Television jargon often says that a variety special is 'showcasing' a certain performer. The showcase is plate glass for an expensive article: a talent has been marketed as a commodity. In the early days of situation comedy, characters too were the obedient servants of the consumer items which sponsored them. In *The Goldbergs*, a comedy about a Jewish family in the Bronx, Mrs Goldberg would occasionally aim her chubby person across the window sill, as if reaching from the box's interior into our living room, to recommend us to buy Sanka brand, which, she said, kept Mr Goldberg even-tempered. Her aim was to make the house in which we watched her a replica of the studio set in which she performed, its pantry stocked with the same items. Sometimes – so concerned are we to adjust differences between our domestic comfort and those of the television characters who are our exemplars – the traffic of recommendation and charitable donation has moved in the opposite direction. Viewers were dismayed by the tacky Brooklyn apartment of Jackie Gleason and his wife in *The Honeymooners* with its derelict fittings and soiled furniture, and they posted curtains and articles of clothing to the character played by Audrey Meadows.

All television's sets are shops: every prop is purchasable. Another of the 1950s situation comedies, *Ozzie and Harriet*, was sponsored by Hotpoint electrical appliances and as a result many of the episodes took place in the kitchen, where the company's products were on show. Later the backer changed to Listerine: that company tried (without success) to shift the action to the bathroom, and pleaded with Ozzie and Harriet to gargle once in a while on camera. When Lucille Ball and Desi Arnaz acquired a house in Palm Springs, they stocked it free of charge by volunteering to endorse the products they coveted.

Here was one of consumerism's gaudy dreams at work: you can requisition goods by the mere act of praising them.

Though Lucille Ball could when it suited her truckle to a sponsor, her series *I Love Lucy* is an inspired and antic mockery of consumerism. Her comic persona belongs specifically on television, because it's devised as a defamation of those serenely competent home-makers on the ads, soaps and sitcoms. For Lucy, the consumer items which the other women tend and treasure are enemies, booby traps and gruesome practical jokes. Her comic routines are always case studies of consumer havoc – a deranged commentary on the technologically eased and pacified world of the ads. She buys a worthless vacuum cleaner from a treacherous salesman, gets herself locked in a freezer, or is carted off in a garbage can. Playing at being a pioneer wife, she bakes her own bread and adds so much yeast that a loaf eight-feet long protrudes from her oven; she also laboriously churns her own butter at a cost, in 1952, of $23.75 a pound. In industry she does no better, devastating a chocolate factory. Assigned to wrapping by her desperate employers, she can't keep pace with the conveyor belt so stuffs the excess chocs into her mouth and various coigns of her costume, a gluttonously literal parody of the consumer in action. To stimulate the growth of her husband's hair, she unleashes a domestic arsenal which alarmingly mocks the remedies deployed by her colleagues on the ads – vibrators, mustard plaster, a plunger and a heat cap to bake the goo she whips up on his scalp.

The angelic heroines of consumerism make homes by assembling all the articles the ads have instructed them to buy. Lucy on the contrary is a demented home-wrecker. To rid herself of a maid, she makes her house such a mess that the maid, she hopes, will be provoked to quit of her own accord. Chickens run riot through her living room when the photographers from *House and Garden* arrive to commemorate her interior decor. Dramatising her desire to move from New York to the suburbs, she powders a room with talcum to represent dust; when she wants to change to another apartment in the same building, her tactic is to congest the rooms with junk to make Ricky think the place is claustrophobic. Her washing machine erupts. She ransacks and ruins the furniture of her neighbours, the Mertzes, while helping them paint and redecorate. She dismantles a brick barbecue because she thinks her wedding ring is lodged in the cement. Her misadventures sabotage the relationship of trust and affection consumerism exerts itself to create between products and their purchasers. In one episode, she makes a commercial for a potion called Vitameatavegin but, sampling the product while rehearsing her inane sales talk, gets drunk because the tonic is 23 per cent alcohol. In another, she markets her recipe for salad-dressing on television and is inundated with orders she can't fill. Finding she is losing money anyway, she goes back on television to denounce her own product as poison. Most blasphemously of all, she slanders a sponsor. Ricky's new show is being broadcast live from their apartment, but Lucy imagines they're only rehearsing and cheerfully libels the department store which is sponsoring the event: she comes in to breakfast complaining of the concrete Phipps mattress on their bed, spurns the Phipps food she's offered, and sports a sack to disparage its clothing department. Her ravaging of consumerism extends naturally into a campaign against television. Ricky's fiddling with the dials causes the Mertzes' set to blow up; Fred, retaliating, kicks in Ricky's television. To stop their husbands watching the sports programmes, she and Ethel cut the antenna wires on the roof of their apartment house. Lucille Ball is television's indigenous anarchist, who jeers hilariously at the medium and wrecks the economy which supports it.

8
News

Each of television's genres, though deferring to the world outside the set, is actually self-reflecting. The medium refracts the realities in which it deals, scaling them down and locking them inside the box which is their theatre. The medium will only tolerate things if they can be made televisual. Talk on television, for instance, is meant to be seen not heard. Nixon in the 1960 presidential campaign debates with Kennedy suffered not because of the frailty of his arguments but because of the insecurity of his image. With his rigid but fidgety posture, he was too devious and complicated to be contained by the bland small screen, and too perturbingly real – where else but on television would his five-o'clock shadow have been held against him? In the Chicago debate of 26 September, television paid him a back-handed compliment. It conferred on him the discreet low definition which is the medium's approved style and which he so plaintively needed, but in the process it made him vanish. Nixon had ill-advisedly worn a grey suit, and as a result he decomposed on the screen, merging into the dots and dashes which compose the television image.

The programme genres I have so far discussed are all commentaries on the medium. The amnesia which is an occupational hazard of soap opera characters is also a quality of television itself; the locations of the serials – hospital wards, bars, motels – are places of transit yet scenes of helpless claustration, surrogates for the television set. The game shows and commercials are the medium's mercenary propaganda for itself, reminders that watching television is sedentary window-shopping. People too (as a later chapter on drama will argue) are made to fit the medium's version of reality, re-formed either as angelically characterless ciphers or as opprobrious stereotypes. The television actor cedes his personal identity to the medium, and if he battles to recover it he may find that it no longer exists.

Television's deftest alteration of content to match its hermetic, transistorised form occurs with the news. As we watch, reality is remade as televisual fiction. For, rather than reporting the news, television's presumption is to invent it. The news on television isn't hearsay, relayed to us by an impartial messenger. It happens at the medium's instigation, for the cameras are no longer obsequious witnesses but agents of provocation. The demonstrators raise their voices and their clenched fists when the cameras arrive. The newsman won't scruple to incite a media event if it seems reluctant to occur. Gary Paul Gates – in his account of CBS television news, *Air Time* – describes an adventurer who, hastening to New Jersey to film what he hoped would be a prison riot, found only a mild ruckus, which had already been pacified. The prison authorities at first refused to admit the cameras, knowing they could easily reignite the protest. Eventually they relented, but still would not allow the crew direct access to the prisoners. The news team therefore went sedately about its business, preparing to film some indifferent and inactive convicts. Then, when all was ready, the reporter in charge signalled to the prisoners with a raised arm and a single extended finger in a gesture of scabrous disdain. They of course co-operated by staging a noisy riot for the cameras.

The newsmen can't be entirely blamed for their aggravation

of events, because their methods are licensed by the politicians, diplomats and terrorists who are their subjects. These people believe in their own actions only if they can see them on television, and have therefore taken to negotiating not with government agents or officials but with the cameramen. The revolutionary leaders of Iran snubbed American diplomats and chose the network correspondents as channels of communication. Access to television is a motive for committing terrorist outrages. The gunmen who commandeered the Iranian Embassy in London in the spring of 1980 wanted publicity for their cause. The cameras, massed on a podium of scaffolding across the street, at once gratified them, and the gunmen passed the time inside the building watching their own siege on the television news. As the days went by, a dispute arose between those who regarded the stand-off as a media event and those who were concerned not with its factitious drama but with the release of the hostages. One of the news networks squabbled with the police, who wouldn't allow the cameras behind the building, where they might have alerted the terrorists to the rooftop preparations for an invasion. A camera was smuggled past the barrier, and did film the paratroopers planning their assault, though these pictures were suppressed until after the siege had ended.

The newsmen in London attempted to requisition the event and convert it to their own purposes. The police, they felt, were an obstruction and a nuisance, interfering with their right to pursue – and if necessary foment – a story. The television newsman embodies the hubris of his medium at its most alarming. His professional arrogance entitles him to assume control of the event he's supposed to be watching. Sometimes (as at the New Jersey prison) he conjures up news; on other occasions he smothers it just by being there, and instead reports on the intrepidity of his own reporting. The two presidential conventions of 1980 were comic cases of the medium's frustration of the events it believed it was sponsoring. In Detroit, the rumoured collaboration of Reagan and Gerald Ford was the wishful thinking of the reporters, but their zeal in promoting it prevented it from actually happening. Upstairs in his hotel suite, Reagan watched Ford employing the television newsmen as his unwitting brokers and stalking horses, and made up his mind not to be manipulated. Disconcerted when Reagan's announcement made them retract, the newsmen indignantly insist that they own the occasion, and regard the politicians as intruders. 'It's *our* convention not theirs,' one of the reporters was quoted as remarking in the *New York Times*.

In New York, too, the convergence of 11,500 media people at Madison Square Garden literally choked and halted the consultations of the paltry minority of 3,381 Democratic Party delegates. Each television network despatched teams of snoops to patrol the floor of the hall, where they scouted rumours and fabricated stories about changing allegiances within the state delegations. As a result of their omnipresence, trailing their cables and trundling their equipment, the aisles became so blocked that delegates couldn't move about to do their own business. On the first night of the convention, the reporters paralysed the voting on the rules which they were present, supposedly, to observe. During the first roll-call, the larger delegations had to defer their decision because they had difficulty in rounding up and polling their members. But as each hesitation was announced, the camera crews thrust their way to the scene and further impeded counsel: votes couldn't be counted because inside the stockade of cameras and commentators no one could move.

By such stratagems as these, television has adapted the news to the medium which transmits it. Television's dominant tense is the present. All gratifications must be instant. Cookery demonstrations evince television's unappeasable impatience: a trick of the format is to have a sample of the dish being prepared already cooked and ready to be eaten, so that by the

time the ingredients have been mixed the process is over –
television can't tolerate that anxious interval of waiting, which
it would think of as a dead and empty air. News on television is
no longer a retrospective absorption of what happened during
the day but a breathless report on what's happening at the
moment. Television's ambition is to bring us the news before it
happens. Correspondents at the presidential conventions are
issued with copies of significant speeches hours before they're
delivered. By the time the speech is being made, they have
advanced to the next fancied 'newsbreak'. With Reagan's
choice of a running-mate, they were outguessing the future in
the hope of influencing that future, and for once their impor-
tunings were resisted. ABC News advertises its late night
bulletins by saying that it will report from parts of the world
where – given the time-difference between the United States
and Europe – it's already tomorrow.

The symbol of television news is that stopwatch which ticks
its way relentlessly through CBS's *60 Minutes*. The programme's segments investigate current affairs, and at the end
of each portion, before and after the commercial break, the
hand on the watch dial is seen darting ahead, consigning the
completed segment to the past. The hand's martial advance
towards that zero at the top of the dial from which it set out is
the rhythm of television news. The evening news compresses a
day around the world into half an hour, and the editors, in
planning each night's broadcast, grade events by allotting to
each a quotient of valuable seconds. Those seconds are the
disputed domain of the newsmen, who beg for more generous
helpings of time in which to develop their stories. Working
against the stopwatch both in the preparation and the delivery
of their reports, they have developed a sense of time which is
bizarrely spatial. Their jargon testifies to this. The host of the
first hour of afternoon news on channel 4 in New York, Chuck
Scarborough, used to open the way for his successor, who
unveiled the headlines at 6 p.m., by promising that 'Tom

Snyder will be here at the top of the hour.' The tolling of the hour is a summit, down from which the broadcast will progressively slide into triviality, and Snyder, at least in Scarborough's view, is an alpinist, hanging high in space because he has been allocated an enviable, exposed moment in time. At the end of the evening broadcast, an announcer used to declare 'this *has been* the CBS evening news with Walter Cronkite.' That abrupt lapse into the preterite signifies that the day, having been parcelled up by the programme, is now done with, as disposable as yesterday's newspaper. The same expulsion from giddy present to obscure and unlamented past sometimes overtakes the newsreaders along with the news. While Cronkite was on holiday in 1971, CBS replaced him with a correspondent called John Hart. This was Hart's brief span of celebrity on camera and, at the end of his last broadcast on the evening before Cronkite's return, he read his own obituary: 'I *was* John Hart,' he told the viewers.

Given television's hectic, peremptory present, the emphasis in its news reporting has shifted from the significance of events to their currency. The only way television can cope with the past is to update it, or to restage it as if it were the present. During the 1950s, television indeed set out to reorganise the world's long and dreary history into its own continuous, happening-jammed present, by sending a newsman (Walter Cronkite) to report on the fall of Troy or the assassination of Caesar or the signing of the Declaration of Independence as if they were contemporary headlines. On *You Are There*, the events were re-enacted as a costume drama while Cronkite, in civvies, wandered among the performers, sagely pausing to interview the wrathful Achilles or Jefferson and his colleagues. The absurdity of the notion concealed a serious point: this was journalism interrogating and vanquishing history, depriving the past of its integrity and its completion, demanding that its characters relocate themselves in the 1950s. Television packages and appraises individual histories according to a similar logic in *This is Your Life*. The past of the subject is, as we watch, exhumed, restored to the present. Long-lost or long-forgotten mentors and associates are heard as offstage voices and then suddenly appear before us. Like *You Are There*, this is the televisual opposite of history and memory: it's not the present meditatively revisiting and re-examining the past but the past gratuitously, often dismayingly, reincarnated in the present. No wonder the subjects of *This is Your Life* have to be surprised, lured into the studio on false pretences to be confronted with a past they thought they'd lived down. Some of them (Mohammed Ali, for instance) don't bother to conceal their annoyance at this forced resuscitation of their past; others (like Lord Mountbatten) nobly manage to forgive the impertinence. At the end of a *This is Your Life* episode, the subject is handed a volume containing his life: a collection of snapshots in which all periods of that life televisually coexist. Television technology has devoted itself to finding new ways of perpetuating the present. The sports programmes, for instance, are able to decelerate the garbled moment of a game (in slow motion) or regurgitate them (in action replays).

Encroaching on the news, television has reorganised it visually. At first, the news was read. Now it's shown. The change began when the networks started experimenting with static illustrations – graphic diagrams, maps, still photographs; technology made it easier, first with videotape and satellites for beaming reports across continents, then with the invention of the minicam, which transmits images directly to the studio by microwave, eliminating the time which formerly had to be allowed for film processing. The newsman's deadline is advanced by the minicam. He no longer needs a reflective pause between the making of his report and the broadcast but can be seen on location with his story during the broadcast, performing in the dare-devil present tense by which television is exhilarated. The medium has been so successful in imposing its own values on the news that even reporters who have nothing to show us flinch from the indignity of merely telling their stories and insist on being seen posed in the places from which they're reporting. The White House correspondents of the American networks shiver or sweat in all weathers on the lawn outside that building to record their evening commentaries. They're not allowed inside, where the stories lurk, and there's nothing to look at except the architecture, but the television newsman has to demonstrate some visual credential. Dan Rather, CBS's sentinel on that lawn during the Johnson and Nixon tenancies of the White House, impressed his audience as much for his hardihood in braving the temperatures as for his enterprise in reporting: viewers would often write in or telephone, wondering about his health.

This concern to give every report some certificate of visual authenticity has become one of the medium's queerest clichés. It tempts television to appraise all events touristically, to turn the news story into a picture postcard. To take a case at random – on 29 April 1980 the BBC news included a report on the European reaction to Mrs Thatcher's intransigence at the EEC summit over British budget payments. We were shown a newsman standing on a Paris street holding three French daily papers and paraphrasing the headlines in which they denounce Mrs Thatcher. His evidence was textual (the newspapers), yet he felt compelled to present it visually. Why did we need to see the papers in his hand, since we weren't reading them but being told about them? What did the location contribute to his report? It worked, in fact, to subvert the news to which it was supposedly an innocuous backdrop. Rather than listening, we look around for intriguing local irrelevancies behind the reporter – people in berets loitering at the news kiosk, Citroëns speeding by. The visuals have taken over from the reporter and trivialised him: he's now just a man in a foreign place, despatching greetings to those at home.

Television news often prefers non-events. The visual highlights of the Democratic Convention in August 1980 were the

refusal of Edward Kennedy to hug Jimmy Carter in concilia-
tion on the platform, and the failure of one of the caches of
balloons strung in the auditorium roof to open and litter the
jubilant crowd with its contents. A few days later Billy Carter
came to New York to testify before a federal grand jury on his
Libyan connections. He avoided the newsmen outside the
courthouse, entering the building another way. Refusing to be
balked, the midday news on channel 9 showed the ranks of
disappointed cameramen still on duty outside, making a story
from the absence of a photographic story. The trailer for the
evening bulletin teased us with the possibility of another
non-event: 'Will Billy Carter appear on camera tonight?' His
evasion of the cameras was enough, for these television journalists, to incriminate him. Two days later, on 28 August, I
saw a reporter on the channel II *Action News* from New York
hypocritically affecting to pray for a non-event. The story was
action news with a vengeance. A young homosexual navy
veteran had jumped to his death from the window of a San
Francisco office building. He had designed his demise as a
media event, addressing his suicide note – a confession of his
sexual misery and sense of defeat – 'To the press'. Having
smashed the window, he hesitated on the sill for three hours,
while friends and policemen pleaded with him, and while the
cameras watched from the street below. Then he jumped. The
female reporter on the scene said 'we all hoped' he'd yield to
persuasion and return to safety. Yet her very presence there
with the camera gave the lie to this sentiment: if he hadn't
jumped, there'd have been no story. She had an interest in his
death, and to capitalise on it, the bulletin showed his leap twice
over, the second time in slow motion like the action replay of a
virtuoso goal in a football match.

Action news specialises in showing the reporter at work
stalking his story, rather than telling us what that story is. A
New York station boasts of the fact that its newsmen walk to
the office: they aren't detached consciences presiding over and

pacifying a disturbed world (which was Cronkite's role at CBS) but members of the community they investigate; the streets are to them a beat and a personal fief as well as a professional assignment. Action news despatches its reporters in convoys to penetrate the city's dark places – burning tenements, the street corners and dingy bars where prostitutes solicit and drugs are traded, the sordid rooms where murders are committed – and then reassembles them in the safety of the newsroom where, like travellers at last returning home from a perilous journey, they tell their gruesome tales to the anchorman. The reports often concentrate on the vicissitudes of the newsmen not their successes. We see the reporters being jostled, heckled, obstructed, and the jumpy hand-held camera vouches for the dangers and discomforts they intrude on. The television newsman has assumed the role of urban vigilante, nocturnal prowler through the jungle of cities, which formerly belonged to the private eye. Like the private eye, he often stumbles into disfavour with the law. Perhaps the television newsmen are so proprietorial about political conventions because they remember them as personal combat-zones, where the fearlessly inquisitive reporters clashed with the fixers for whom the cameras were trespassing. At the 1964 Republican Convention, John Chancellor of CBS was arrested on camera for his intrusion into the party's secret conclaves, and signed off hurriedly, saying 'this is John Chancellor, somewhere in custody'; and in 1968 in Chicago, Dan Rather was beaten up by Mayor Daley's henchmen.

American television celebrates its newsmen (and thereby displaces attention from the news which it's their job to gather) by according them its moral esteem, whether as totems of paternal trust like Cronkite or as feisty partisans of truth like Rather. The reporter has reserved to himself a power superior to that over which the politicians bicker, for he can both make governments and – since Watergate – unmake them. Cronkite symbolically performed the first of these offices, Rather the second. Announcing his retirement as anchorman in February 1980, Cronkite employed a phrase which sums up the conceit of authority with which television beguiles the newsreader. He explained that he would desist only after the presidential inauguration in January 1981, because 'I've inaugurated every President since Harry Truman, and I want to do one more.' He meant that he'd reported on those inaugurations, but his choice of words confided his view of himself: he is a head of state who lends legitimacy to the elected officials by condescending to describe their activities. There is even a certain truth to his assumption. For who would know that a president had been inaugurated unless the occasion were shown on television? The ceremony is staged for television; television is therefore entitled to consider itself the power which ordains the ceremony. Rather, Cronkite's successor on the CBS evening news, embodies a different conception of the reporter's power. If the newsman can grant legitimacy to an executive, as Cronkite imagines he did at those inaugurations, he can also revoke it. Rather did so in an angry exchange with Nixon at a press conference in Houston during March 1974. When he stood up to ask his question, there were flurries of applause and booing from the other broadcasters present. Nixon, accustomed by then to Rather's aggressiveness, asked him, 'Are you running for something?' Rather shot back, 'No, sir, Mr President – are you?' The reply was a small miracle of improvised insolence, for it disputed Nixon's authority and even his right to cavil at the interviewer's persecution of him. Barbara Walters devised for herself a complementary persona. If the men were the scourges of the powerful, defiantly outfacing them, her role would be that of maternal intercessor, wheedlingly mitigating authority by her pleas for mercy. Interviewing President Carter and his wife, she concluded by begging them, 'Be good to us, be kind to us.'

At his most insanely self-deluded, the newsman can imagine that reading the news endows him with a special prescience, and can begin decreeing solutions to the problems he reviews in the broadcasts. This was the case with Dave Garroway, compere during the 1950s on *The Today Show*. He was forever warning his viewers of the communist calamity which was about to overcome them, and accusing news agencies of treason. Cronkite, more cautiously, sees the newsman's power as one of superintendence not remonstration or intervention. In May 1980 it was rumoured that Cronkite might agree to become the vice-presidential running-mate of the independent candidate John Anderson. Cronkite gravely discounted the possibility, in terms which made it clear that political office would be a demotion when compared with his honorific eminence on the CBS news. He hoped, he said, that journalists would not succumb to 'the political bug'. The reporter's most precious attribute is his 'credibility', which he 'holds in trust'. To squander that serene impartiality by aligning himself with a single political group would 'degrade what he has been'. Behind the logic of this renunciation lies Cronkite's mystic alternative to the American constitution: the head of state, symbolising the continuity of the nation, is the anchorman, and the politicians derive their tenure and their legality from him.

Why should Cronkite trifle with a candidacy for vice-president when he'd already, as a newsman, succeeded in abashing an elected president? For it is alleged that Lyndon Johnson only accepted that the Vietnam war was unwinnable when Cronkite told him so on the evening news. Cronkite was at first an apologist for that military adventure. He visited Vietnam in 1965 and returned convinced of the war's moral justice and confident that it was being swiftly and efficiently prosecuted. In 1968 he made a second trip, and this time saw the sorry and chaotic truth. He felt personally piqued, as if the government and its warriors had set out to dupe him with their optimistic rhetoric. This sense of betrayal is a symptom of newsman's hubris – Cronkite had shared this misjudgment with millions of others; but in his case the error was a crime, because it had shown his vaunted credibility to be no more than ordinary credulity. He therefore, when back in New York, instructed the government 'to negotiate, not as victors, but as an honourable people who lived up to their pledge to defend democracy, and did the best they could.' To Johnson, Cronkite's disillusionment with the war represented the failure of national consensus, and soon afterwards he announced that he would not seek re-election. Later that year at the Chicago convention Cronkite again threatened the unruly politicians with excommunication, as if he could invalidate their dealings by ceasing to report them. When Dan Rather was assaulted, Cronkite included a glowering reprimand to Daley in his broadcast: 'if this sort of thing continues, it makes us, in our anger, want to just turn off our cameras and pack up our microphones and get the devil out of this town.'

Despite Cronkite's mock-modest disclaimers, it's his career which sums up television's modifications of the news it reports. For he, like television itself, is a medium who doesn't so much transmit messages as deflect, sedate and atone for them. More than reading the news, he certifies its veracity, lending it that credibility which is less a product of his journalistic skill than of his silver-haired, mild-toned, homey image. At the 1952 conventions CBS devised the name 'anchorman' for the function he performed – a point of referral, connecting and interpreting the contradictory reports from the floor. Subsequently, the anchor changed from a journalistic convenience to a symbolic necessity. His reassuring presence made bad news less alarming. Cronkite attended carefully to the cultivation of this image, aware of its importance in palliating the news. During the credits at the end of a broadcast he would often relax and take out his pipe, revolving it meditatively in his hand. He never smoked it on camera, but simply placed it in evidence as an emblem, an item in his equipment as national paterfamilias. So successfully did he upstage the news (with which he shortly got equal billing: his programme was called, even when he wasn't there to anchor it, *The CBS Evening News with Walter Cronkite*) that the tragedies and conquests of the past two decades are remembered with reference to his comportment when describing them on the air. The assassination of John Kennedy cathartically shattered that imperturbable image. Hastening to the studio, Cronkite had no time to put on a jacket or arrange his hair; when he announced the president's death, his voice faltered and he shed tears. For the moonshot in 1969, Cronkite regressed into a small boy agog at the working of machines, cheering the technological triumph in enthusiastic baby talk. 'Go, baby, go!' he yelped when the rocket was launched, and he blessed the landing with pious banality: 'Man finally standing on the surface of the moon. My golly!' Since Cronkite's accustomed position was behind the desk as the unmoved mover of the news, he could create a small sensation merely by standing up. He did so during a programme on Watergate in 1972, leaving the chair which was his point of anchorage to fiddle with some diagrams illustrating the investigation. In getting up, he became a partisan, and persuaded viewers of the seriousness of the investigation. Early on, Cronkite coined a slogan for himself, with which he signed off each night: 'And that's the way it is,' he would tell his public. Over the years, this tag became a rite, a melioristic assurance. The way it was had – it was implied – Cronkite's approval. During his final year he augmented his daily leave-taking by adding the date to his slogan and computing the number of days the American hostages had now spent in capitivity in Tehran. Keeping this daily tally, he was acting both as the nation's archivist, counting time for it, and as its unsleeping conscience.

The British are more irreverent about those who read the news to them, but no less worshipful. In Britain the news-readers endear themselves not by their Cronkite-like moral worth but by their raffishness. The more they're chattered about in the salacious press, the more popular they become. Gossip – speculation about Anna Ford's marital projects or Reginald Bosanquet's night-clubbing – is the source of their authority. There's a jolly tribal solidarity to British smut. Nothing is sacred, because everything is in the family. Even the BBC is Auntie, a pompous, old-fashioned lady who can be giggled at but never disowned. Thus whereas American television sanctifies its newsreaders, the British public cheekily wants to know what goes on under the desk. The starchy Angela Rippon entered the national consciousness only when she bared her legs to dance with Morecambe and Wise on their Christmas show, exposing, quite literally, what the newsdesk concealed.

Bulletins in the two countries have a quite different character. The American networks employ the news to dramatise television's own technological omniscience. ABC for instance divides its programme between three continent-spanning studios in New York, Chicago and London. From the first, American television prided itself on its elimination of estranging distances. The medium was a communicator. In 1951 a coaxial cable knit together the continent, an instant, airy successor to the railways which connected the coasts in the previous century. Television celebrated the feat in a CBS programme called *See It Now*, vaulting live from the Golden Gate to the Brooklyn Bridge, traversing the country in the time it took to replace one image with another. The choice of the two bridges as inaugural images for the cable was significant. Those heroic trajectories of steel were the products of an earlier age's ambition to communicate. They abolish distance materially. But the coaxial cable and the microwave relay accomplished the same victory over space electronically. The American news programmes continue to aspire to this instant incorporation of the world. Their decor alludes to the simultaneity in time of all the world's separate locations, with walls of clocks adjusted to the correct hours for the cities of all continents. Their urgent background music is the chatter of the teletype machines, disgorging information from all these remote centres.

British television has never had this ambition to unify the world by satellite, to use the medium as a means of global surveillance and therefore of global reconciliation. Within its more manageable national space, its news bulletins cosily confirm tribal unity. The broadcasts are constructed so as to absorb the news into the safe, enduring community which its alarms and surprises might seem to menace. The bulletins begin with the day's calamities – terrorist attacks or strikes. Both are suited to, perhaps staged for, television. Terrorism is gratuitous violence: havoc and murder as theatre, played out for the cameras. When television euphemises a strike as 'industrial action', it makes of it a media event, promoting inertia to an active status: the television cameras cue the marchers to chant and the pickets to close ranks. After this fabrication of disasters, the bulletins gently subside into familial comedy. As a rule the editors reserve for the final story in the BBC news some un-newsworthy anecdote about animals or amiable eccentrics or members of the royal family. The purpose of this item is folksy homage to the national character. It may take the form of a lying-in at the London zoo, or the panic of gardeners at the Chelsea flower show about slugs on their orchids. Politicians, whose activities are chronicled soberly at the beginning of the broadcast, have by the end settled into family elders, vexatious but lovable uncles and aunties. On 28 May 1980, for instance, the last item in the BBC bulletin was an encounter at Madame Tussaud's between Mrs Thatcher and a new wax replica of herself. The original was overheard querulously wondering why the wax-workers hadn't given the dummy an engagement ring. During the broadcast, she had slid from a political agent to a comic ogre in a national institution. The decline isn't derisive: it simply vouchsafes her membership of the family. The week before, a bulletin concluded with a small moral fable about tribal generosity, an account of the letters, cards and gifts arriving at Catford police station for the young constable whose hand was blown off by a bomb planted there a few days earlier. While he recovers in hospital, £25,000 has been received in donations from sympathetic members of the public. When he was a tragic victim, at the time of the blast, he was at the head of the news; now his place was at the end, in a redemptive epilogue; later in the year, when deprived of his job, he edged back towards the top, since he was again a hapless sacrifice. If the final item has been comic, the newsreader is permitted a shyly inept flippancy of his own; if it has been a homey parable, he will beam genially.

Television's arrogation of the news is summed up in a single, unobtrusive prop. Angela Rippon, during bulletins on BBC2, often brandished in her right hand a silver-plated ball-point pen, which was there not to be used but to signify that she'd been caught in the act of writing – or inventing – the news she was merely reading. This professional self-conceit has infected those close colleagues of the newsreaders, the weathermen. Egged on by the narcissism of their medium, they occasionally seem to believe that they've made the weather they're describing. In predicting how it will turn out tomorrow they speak, like soothsayers, as if they were determining it. An example, at station-hopping random. The BBC's lugubrious weatherman on 30 June 1980 shrugged his shoulders at us and said, 'As you'll see I've had to cover pretty much the whole of the country with rain.' He was referring to the black cut-out clouds he'd scattered in a flotilla across the map, but his way of saying it betrayed his televisual conviction of his own power: it had been his decision to decree the rain.

The American weathermen aren't so glumly oracular as those retained by the BBC. On the contrary, they see it as their responsibility to merchandise the weather. On the channel 11 news from New York on 15 August 1980, the weatherman served up the weekend's promised temperatures to us as a commodity, enthusiastically scouting its advantages as if expecting us to buy it from him. That most perishable of items, the weather, had become another of the consumer durables which it's the function of commercial television to sell. 'We've got a lovely package of weather shaping up for you,' he announced. The figure of speech tells all: the studio is a factory where the weather's concocted, before it's distributed across the country to be put on display in those domestic retail outlets which are our television sets. Giftwrapping the weather, television makes it synonymous with the men who prognosticate about it. One of the New York stations has a weatherman whose name qualifies him as a virtual weathervane. He's called Storm Field, but that louring designation is contradicted by a toothy smile ('worth 200G a year', according to a news story about him) which is an ersatz sunburst.

Though the anchor must be a sage, the weatherman is, on American television, more often a comedian. The former has to be believed; but it would be better if we didn't believe the latter, since he's likely to daunt our optimism. The weatherman therefore embraces his own ignominy by behaving as if his were a ludicrous calling. On 'happy talk' news programmes, the weatherman is the smirking butt of his colleagues' taunts and puns. 'Where do weathermen keep their money?' we're asked. The answer is, 'In cloud-banks.' The weathermen appear inanely garbed for the temperatures they're predicting, or draw cartoons of shivering or sweating puppets on their satellite maps. Why these antics? Once more, it's the medium's compulsory palliation of its messages. Perhaps the weathermen remember as their disreputable ancestors those false prophets, the rainmakers. Or perhaps they're embarrassed by the weather which is their subject. The British derive a stoic consolation from the soggy equanimity of their weather. Every night on the BBC we're reassured that tomorrow will be a damp and arthritic extension of today. But Americans long to overcome the inclemencies of the weather.

Gene Kelly did so by singing in the rain. The weathermen do so by apologetically euphemising the dreaded rain as 'probability of precipitation'. On one ugly occasion, the weatherman's ideology of Panglossian uplift spilled over the border into the sombre reality of the news. The ABC station in New York had a story during November 1976 about the rape of an eight-year-old girl. This item was followed by the weather forecast. Tex Antoine the weatherman evidently felt it his professional obligation to be as blithe and comically resilient about the assault as he always was about the weather. He therefore suggested that the viewers should consider 'the words of Confucius: "If rape is inevitable, lie back and enjoy it".' His gruesome sally cost him his job, but it can be recorded as another moment of televisual hubris, like Cronkite's remark about inaugurating presidents: a declaration of form's victory over content, elevating the man who reads the news to the head of state and the man who forecasts the weather to his alter ego, the saturnalian court jester.

9
Drama

Television's imperative is to fill up time – to occupy the hours allotted to it by the schedules, and to perform the same service for its listless, leisured viewers. Drama is therefore wherever possible serial, carrying within itself a reason for its extrapolation. But not for continuing, as a narrative does, in order to complete an action. The structure of a television series belies the continuity which is its professed aim. Each episode has to be complete in itself, and a season's programmes comprise a file of separate anecdotes, adventures or investigations. You're kept watching from week to week not by suspense but by habit. The format of the series reckons on the fickleness and dozy inattention of the viewers, who are never required to retain anything from the previous week's instalment. How could they be? Such a demand would contravene the nature of television itself, which so hastily erases its tapes, effaces its yesterdays, and prefers repetition (as of commercials) to development. The only continuous thing about a series is its weekly time-slot. It's this – a location in the schedules and in the routine of the viewers – which gives a series its identity: positioning in television's private time and space, not content. Television's genres are its various time-zones. The nature of a series is determined by the hour at which it's meant to be transmitted. The early evening is for situation comedies; later on, crime and detection are the permitted subjects. Programmers superstitiously maintain that an alteration in scheduling can exterminate a show. Game shows, for instance, are supposed to be bad risks in the afternoon. Their competitive commercial hysteria suits the energetic, optimistic morning; dreary afternoon is sacred to the soaps.

Far from being inhibited by these formal limitations – the collapse of a series into a folio of separable episodes; the reliance on inert habit rather than the curiosity and commiseration which keep people interested in narratives – television embraces them. Think of how it treats character. In a play, character is fate: a determination of will which explodes into action, which instigates the drama and impels it to an end – Macbeth's vaulting ambition, for instance. In a novel, character isn't so propulsive or predestinate: character here is consciousness exploring itself, diverging and detouring, like Tristram Shandy perambulating inside his own head or Leopold Bloom strolling through Dublin. Whether in a play or a novel, however, character is powered by a logic of its own – impatiently active in the one, meditatively arrested in the other. But the peculiarity of character on television is that it's devised and motivated not in obedience to psychological propriety but in accordance with needs and calculations which are external to it. Character on television is form not content.

The medium is ruthlessly opportunistic in its contrivance of destinies for its people. Their histories are governed by the invisible but omnipresent ratings, which decree whether they will live or die, marry or be divorced. The happy endings of television people are manufactured to appease the ratings. When Sonny and Cher were divorced in 1974, he defected to another network, leaving Cher alone for the next season of what had been their joint show. She slumped in the ratings, and to recoup viewers was reunited with Sonny. The fact that she was already expecting the child of her new husband was a mere technicality. The case of Rhoda's terminated marriage is the obverse of that of Sonny and Cher, who were summarily respliced before the cameras, but it proves the same point about television's power over its creatures. Rhoda began as Mary Tyler Moore's neighbour, then graduated to her own show. She owed her promotion to the ratings, and led a charmed life until, in her new series, she got married. Thereafter the writers found it harder to devise stories about her: she was interesting as a wittily aggressive loner, not as a spouse. In 1976 they gained an extension for the guttering show by expelling her husband, sacrificing the luckless Joe to the ratings. Later Rhoda's job (as a window-dresser) was similarly jettisoned. Her success bored the writers who, needing to invent a new motive for her, infected her with their own sense of lassitude and of being at a dead-end. Rhoda suddenly and gratuitously became tired of her work, reneged on contracts with her clients, and determined to choose a new career – only to find herself unemployable. But at least her desperate hustling for a job supplied the writers with pretexts for new stories. She had been made to pay the penalty for the exhaustion of the script men. Yet in this transference of motive there's a certain psychological truth. Rhoda's apparent lack of sufficient reason for altering her life matches the motive-hunting of a motiveless dissatisfaction in Americans approaching middle age, who find themselves unexpectedly weary of their own professional success. Television's conventions are arbitrary and their imposition on characters rude, but all the same they match the conventions by which we conduct our private lives.

Character on television is made in the image of the medium itself. It must be serially adaptable, its motives must be expedient and glibly reversible if convenience dictates. The calamities of television people aren't real diseases but contractual ploys. When a character dies on the soaps, it generally means that the actor has demanded to be written out, having found work elsewhere. Characters are briskly expendable, or ground-

lessly extendable. The spun-off series in which minor characters from one show have another written for them elasticise
their subjects, reconceiving them with a blithe disdain for
psychological continuity. Lou Grant began as a gruff, benign
comic ogre on *The Mary Tyler Moore Show* but, having
advanced to a series of his own, was rewritten as a liberal,
post-Watergate investigative journalist.

At its most craftily complex, television fabricates a supplementary drama from the uncertainties which plague it and
damage its dramatic consistency. *Dallas* had to end its 1979–
80 season spectacularly, and at the same time needed to justify
its continuation. The writers therefore selected the venal
J.R. as their victim, and had him shot in his office by an
unknown assailant. The decision was a reckless and arbitrary
bid for time. In the original scheme, the seasonal climax was to
have been the identification of Pamela Ewing's father, since
earlier in the series it had been improvisatorily decided that she
wasn't the legitimate offspring of the soused Digger Barnes
after all. But the network needed an extra episode, and the
writers in conference therefore decided to execute J.R. They
did so without knowing who to blame for firing the shot. It was
as much an inductive puzzle for them as for the viewers: 'We
said the hell with it, let's shoot him and figure out who did it
later.' On television motives don't deliberatively precede an
action; they're assigned, according to convenience and pro-
fitability, after the event. The assassin's identity, it was decided, wouldn't be revealed until the series resumed in the
autumn of 1980; nor would the producers reveal whether J.R.'s
wounds were to prove fatal. In the gap between the spring and
autumn seasons, the unmotivated twist of the plot unfurled
into a collaborative guessing-game for the viewers. The programme licensed those who watched it to invent continua-
tions. A chain of British betting shops accepted wagers on the
identity of the guilty party, pedantically computing the odds
against each suspect. The BBC promoted a competition invit-

ing viewers to unriddle the mystery, and offered as a prize a voyage from fact into fiction: a week in Dallas. As the book-makers adjusted probabilities and the BBC searched out the most meticulously reasoned explanation of the attack, *Dallas* turned into an exemplary case of television's aleatory muta-tion of drama. Its action had been temporarily handed over to the viewers: they could attribute motives to the characters and project futures for the series. The necessity and inevitability which supervise the action of drama had been dethroned, and replaced by whim, guess, and the suppositious arc of the gambler's dice.

Realising this, a firm specialising in war-games marketed a ludic *Dallas* do-it-yourself kit. '*Dallas*: The Television Role-Playing Game' disassembles the series and parcels it up as sociological poker. The game enables its players both to act out the fantasy ('you actually take on the attributes and abilities of one of the nine major characters') and to control it by regulating the action ('one player assumes the role of the Director') or devising new and unanticipated episodes. Each main character owns a portfolio of extras, whose characters and uses are tabulated on playing cards. Since televisual character is formulaic, these supernumeraries aren't described but reduced numerically to the special interests and psycholo-gical forces which constitute them. The function of some characters is organisational: they're deputies of groups – forgers, environmentalists, Texas Rangers, the Mexican-American Farm Workers' Union, the FBI. In other cases, the pawns are individuals, whose manipulability is calculated with shrewd exactness on their card. Alexis Blancher, an employee of Ewing Oil, is rated along these co-ordinates:

Power	o	Seduction	18/7
Persuasion	15/11	Investigation	19/19
Coercion	9/7	Luck	2

Each main character must persuade, coerce or seduce these ductile supers, piecing together a power bloc. The game supplies three ready-to-play scripts in which these ratios of advantage can be tested. Putative situations are outlined – among them the recovery of a Spanish land grant which threatens to alienate an area of the Ewing ranch and cede it to the Mexican-American community – and each of the principals is equipped with the motive which must rule all his or her decisions in the game. The outcome of these three plots can vary each time the game is played, depending on the skill with which the players respond to its chances and on the quantities of supers they manage to win over. The director introduces an additional uncertainty, since his master script reserves to him a series of surprises which can be dealt to the principals, obstructing them and forcing them to reappraise their tactics. When you tire of the scripts in the box, you can rig up your own. Since it's all a matter of shuffling and combining formulae, the possibilities are infinite: 'extensive support material and guidelines, including 70 suggested plot devices, allow anyone to construct an original episode that will be interesting, unpredictable, and exciting'.

The producers of *Dallas*, in planning the next season, seemed to have adopted the game's rule of randomness. They proposed to film a variety of different solutions to the crime, in which characters would take turns to be J.R's assailant. The choice of the real culprit would be made just before the transmission of the revelatory episode in the third week of the autumn season. The actors whose destinies were being toyed with were excluded from the secret: guilt wasn't something bred in and harboured by a particular character but a bonus to be handed out to the least appropriate, least qualified member of the cast. The dramatic integrity of the series was thus publicly and joyfully flouted. The conjunction of character and action became a game of chance.

But while drama was reorganising itself as a factitious

sweepstake, another, more authentically uncertain drama took over. Disbarred from the confidence of the writers and producers about the show's continuation, the actors retaliated by jeopardising that continuation. During the summer recess, the fiction of *Dallas* merged with fact as the refractory actors refused to sign contracts for the new season unless their salaries were dizzily inflated. Patrick Duffy (Bobby) eventually compromised with the producers; Linda Gray (Sue Ellen) held out longer; most stubbornly rapacious was J.R. (Larry Hagman), who demanded a fee of $100,000 per episode. These contract negotiations, breathlessly reported in the gossip columns, turned into a continuation of *Dallas* by other means. Urged on by mercenary agents, the actors became indistinguishable from the scheming plutocrats they portrayed on the show. 'I mean to cash in on it,' said Larry Hagman of his success as J.R., using for the purpose the covetous accents of J.R. himself. The agency managing the affairs of Linda Gray commented on its wrangling with the producers in an idiom which matched the menacing, innuendo-mined terseness the Ewing Oil executives employ to describe their corporate intrigues: 'We're very close to making a deal – but as yet not quite close enough.'

The few officers of the programme's production company who were privy to the secret of J.R.'s attacker conducted their business with a stealth and shrewdness worthy of their counterparts in the fiction, shredding memos after scanning them and commissioning a varity of decoy scripts with alternative denouements to mislead the inquisitive, tactics which mimic J.R.'s double-dealing. The producers were distributing red herrings, just as J.R. in a recent episode had peddled valueless Asian oil leases to his associates. Speculation about the outcome provoked para-industrial espionage when one of the scripts disclosing the assassin's identity was stolen from the production offices. But the ethics of good citizenship prevailed, and a Los Angeles newspaper returned the script without leaking its contents. So intent was reality on outdoing fantasy that the property-developer who owned the ranch on which the Dallas locations were filmed rejoiced in the equivalent of the oil-strikes which enriched the Ewings: he planned to sell shares in the fantasy, offering packages of South Fork sod at a tariff of $25 per square foot.

With greedy fact overtaking the show's most lurid fiction, the producers reacted by threatening to terminate the fantasy. The survival of J.R. became a clause in the contractual dispute. The fantasy's future depended on the resolution of an impasse in fact. If Larry Hagman moderated his financial demands, J.R. would live; if not, the producers would spite him by sentencing the wounded character to expire. Or else they would resurrect him in the body of another, more compliant actor. Character on television is both plastic and elastic, able to be moulded or elongated into whatever form convenience dictates. Reincarnation is therefore possible. When Francesca James on the soap opera *All My Children* requested her release, her character, Kitty, was abruptly killed off. After a while, however, the actress changed her mind and wanted to rejoin the company. Her demise wasn't held against her. The writers had her reappear as her own, uncannily identical and near-homophonic sister, Kelly. An even odder post-mortem existence was proposed for Hagman: re-embodiment as Robert Culp. During the contractual arguments, the producers hinted that Hagman was disposable, and filmed some additional sequences to make good their threat. According to this provisional sequel, the ambulance ferrying J.R. to the hospital from his office would be wrecked in a traffic accident. The wounded J.R. would be burned beyond recognition, and the plastic surgeons would reconstruct for him a face which was exactly that of Robert Culp. Hagman, appreciating that on television no one is irreplaceable, settled with alacrity. The spin-off to *Dallas* was made, as Hagman's substitute would have been, by grafting. The Ewing relatives of *Knot's Landing* actually predated *Dallas*, though the network hadn't at this stage been interested in them. When *Dallas* succeeded, the writers plastically remodelled the shelved Californian characters and attached them to the Ewings, thus converting a false start into a profitable sequel.

Once the fantasy had become common property, everyone wanted to enrol in it. The real drama was taking place outside the series, not on it. While the actors were striving to live up offstage to the wheeling, dealing cupidity of the characters they played, viewers everywhere were eagerly auditioning for roles on the show. A Dallas sheriff volunteered to exchange his badge for a walk-on role, preferring the show's fiction of power to his own diminished reality. The producers had applied to the Dallas police chief to borrow some officers for an episode. When they were refused, the sheriff of Dallas county, recently defeated at the polls and serving out the fag-end of his term, offered his deputies and their cars. The sheriff contended that the Ewing ranch was sited outside the city limits and therefore within his jurisdiction not that of the police chief, inaugurating a demarcation dispute about a fictional property. He also looked to the programme to supply him with a fictional consolation for his electoral loss of office, retaining an agent to help get him cast as the arresting officer when the killer was at last identified. The show's transmutation of its fictions into fact was abetted by the BBC. Having transmitted the final episode of the series in May 1980, it then re-ran the attempt on J.R.'s life in the news broadcast which followed. Make-believe was thus validated and verified by being made a news item.

Dallas handed over its drama to the viewers. We could operate the knobs and manipulate the fantasy as if we were playing one of those electronic games which can be plugged into our television sets. A series which is dramatically null can keep itself going by fomenting drama off-screen, which often contradicts the sedate fictions of the programme itself. This is the case with *Charlie's Angels*, whose real script writers in its later seasons were the gossip columnists, for their chatter about rivalries and resentments between the actresses infused the series with whatever dramatic interest it possessed. To the insipidity of the programme's stories the gossips added a venomously lively subtext. On screen, the angels co-operated with beatific blandness; off stage, apparently, they were forever squabbling over precedence. The invisible Charlie was the most benign of employers, rewarding his angels with Hawaiian vacations for a mission successfully accomplished; the producers of the show were less indulgent towards their fractious actresses, legally bludgeoning the truant Farrah Fawcett into submission after she'd quit in mid-contract and summarily firing Kate Jackson's replacement, Shelley Hack. As the list of defectors from the programme grew, each girl hired as a substitute arrived ambitious to outdo her predecessor. Cheryl Ladd, filling in for Farrah, wore for her first day at work a T-shirt across which was emblazoned, 'Farrah Fawcett-Minor'. The ladies of course affect to regret or deny the gossip about them. But surely they know that the gossip columnists are the dramatists who outfit them with identities and contrive spicier plots than the detective capers to which they're assigned each week by the producers. Farrah abandoned the series in order, she says, 'to grow'. But when the films in which she'd hoped to do her growing sagged, she found that the gossips were her only remaining constituency. Since her work was no longer newsworthy, her one saleable commodity was her life. The gossips fictionalised that for her, titillatingly inventing love affairs for her to act in and mobilising squads of reporters to torment her with their questions at airports. After a few seasons *Charlie's Angels* existed merely to provoke tattle about the tiffs and huffy walk-outs of its stars. The girls aren't interesting when they're dutifully trying to act but only when – in their offstage spats – they're being themselves.

And what are those selves? The angels deserve their name, for they have an ideal, imperturbable, angelic nonentity. There's nothing to distinguish them from one another except their hair, which is also imperturbable. They possess that special genre of personality which television idolises: they're moulded, it seems, of smooth delectable plastic not human flesh. The programme has relied on their interchangeability to manoeuvre it out of difficulties. Thus, when Farrah absconded, Cheryl Ladd could be grafted on as her sister. Both after all are blondes, and hair-colour is the single concession to individuality made in this angelic televisual idyll of physical perfection. Angeldom is the absence of character, and the plots of *Charlie's Angels* capitalise on this very inadequacy. This is why they rely on undercover assignments. The angels are so glossily, celestially featureless that they can pass for anything, and in the course of their investigations they pretend to different identities in each episode. One week they're raunchy roller disco dancers, the next chaste schoolmarms in a ladies' academy, then truckers flirting with their co-professionals on the citizens' band radio waves. None of these impersonations is particularly convincing, but that's the televisual point. The angels, knowing that all they're required to do is permit the camera to ogle them, give a grudging semblance of acting and trust to their costumes to differentiate one role from another: spangled bikinis when they're disco-dancing, prim tweeds for schoolmarming, plaid shirts for trucking. As models, they are what they wear. Whenever one of them stalks out or is sacked, there is always another exquisitely-coiffed clone in wait to replace her.

The history of the series so far suggests that the replication could go on forever. How many sisters has Farrah? There's no reason to confine the family to Cheryl Ladd. Television indeed trades in lookalikes. Lucille Ball's son in *I Love Lucy* was played by an interchangeable pair of twins. Two were needed because of labour laws which restricted the time infants could spend in front of the camera, and as extra insurance there was a supplementary pair of dolls, which took turns playing the role of Little Ricky during rehearsals or in long shots, when their cries were provided by a vaudevillian stationed in the wings – an early instance of television's tendency to turn out physical duplicates as if on a conveyor belt. The angels can be duplicated because they're not persons but types, offprints from a Californian archetype of pneumatic physical health, an arbitrary selection from the crowds of identically pretty girls who populate the television screen. You can see them parading through the choreographic routines of Busby Berkeley, and he too thought they could be hatched and incubated in factory conditions, sleeping (as in *Dames*) two to a bed in immense dormitories, roused by alarm clocks to bathe and beautify themselves, each exerting herself to look exactly like all the others. Berkeley's dances are industrial assembly-lines which manufacture beauty like any other mass-produced article. The girls in *Gold-diggers of 1933* are as alike as the coins they wear; those at the honeymoon hotel in *Footlight Parade* are all coyly surnamed Smith; those in *Dames* all aspire to resemble Ruby Keeler, whose face is imprinted on the placards they carry. It's the ideological guarantee of the Berkeley musicals that anyone of them could indeed become Ruby Keeler, for stardom depends on the accident of opportunity not on talent. Ruby herself in *42nd Street* goes out a gawky novice to return a star. On television, Berkeley's dream of industrially processed, plastically malleable beauty has come true. Just as the news anchormen are all versions of gruff but reasonable paternal authority (one of them is even allegorically dubbed Harry Reasoner) and the game show hosts are all indistinguishably cheery and ingratiating men of the world, so television's women – the chorines who drape themselves around the game show prizes, the giggling newlyweds who suffer the host's probing, the guest stars and special guest stars who move each week through a brief transit of the sky playing wives or girlfriends or murder victims on the dramatic series and then are erased by eclipse – all belong to Charlie's innumerable reserve of angels.

Television favours types not malformed, unrepeatable individuals because, as the title of *Charlie's Angels* implies, it believes the types to have been made in heaven. If television drama individualises a person, it does so by affixing a gimmick. Having failed to qualify as a type, your only alternative is to be a grotesque. Since television adores characterlessness, it confers dramatic individuality as a wound, a slur, a disability – the shaming stigmatum of deviation from type. Television's cohort of private eyes and detectives are all members of a genre. Their meaning is their typicality. How then do we tell them apart? *Charlie's Angels*, slipping lookalikes into the slots vacated by Farrah or Kate Jackson, suggests that we shouldn't even try to. But the other series persist in individualising their protagonists, and they do so by defaming and uglifying them.

The detectives are synonymous with the oddities or ailments which brand them for their offence against the norm or the type. Telly Savalas as Kojak has a shaved crown, Karl Malden on *The Streets of San Francisco* a bifurcated warty nose, Cannon is lumberingly fat, Columbo is a scruff. These physical impediments mark individuality as arbitrary and gimmicky, the badge of an obnoxious or endearingly childish habit, like the gooey lollypops Kojak sucks or the glasses of milk Bubby Ebsen rustically quaffs as Barnaby Jones. Like motive in the soaps, individuality on television is not something you acquire of your own accord but something inflicted on you more or less at random. For some of the detectives it's quite literally an illness. They have only their medical conditions to differentiate them – Raymond Burr as Ironside confined to his wheelchair, David Janssen as Harry Orwell painfully struggling along with a bullet lodged in his back, Ben Gazzara on *Run For Your Life* left by some dread contagion with only two years to live (though NBC presumably secured him a remission, since his series ran for three seasons). If the detectives aren't themselves gimmicky then they're lodged inside a gimmick as their habitat, and this too is an eyesore – the dilapidated red speedster in which Starksy and Hutch cruise their beat, James Garner's trailer in *The Rockford Files* parked on the beach at Malibu to the disgust of the neighbours, whose view it mars.

Opposed to these lamed or derelict detectives are the sleek guest (or special guest) stars who each week play the villains. Despite the billing, these are nobodies or at best has-beens, but their lustrous anonymity and their repeatability constitute for television a standard against which the transgressions of the ill-mannered or overweight or unkempt detectives can be measured. For the detectives, in being reduced to an opprobrious individuality, are being pilloried and disarmed. The investigators are social outlaws, excluded by their coarseness or their illness or their age (Helen Hayes and Mildred Natwick played two superannuated sleuths on *The Snoop Sisters*) or their rural naivety (Barnaby Jones is a Beverly Hillbilly who has improbably set up in business as a private eye; Dennis Weaver as McCloud is disoriented and ill-at-ease, having been transplanted from New Mexico to New York) from the affluent, beautiful world they're scrutinising. Additionally, they're weakened by being scrupulously segregated from the police. Charlie has rescued his angels from the drab chores with which they were burdened after graduation from the police academy; Rockford quarrels with the cops; Starsky and Hutch work within the force but according to their own unorthodox methods, and they disdain uniform. As well as demeaning its detectives (in the case of the gimmick-afflicted men) or nubilely trivialising them (in the case of the angels), television comfortingly renders them ineffective. It takes over the punitive formula of the detective drama, in which the investigator disinters the crimes sheltered by large fortunes, and turns that formula inside out. Now the detective isn't a vigilant conscience disassembling a society predicated on greed and corruption; television makes him an unmannerly and unavailing intruder into the complacent affluence which television itself both represents and defends. On television the detective story changes from a fable of social retribution to a fantasy of social consolidation, because the location of every television show is the idyllic middle-class living room in which it's viewed, and here it's the detectives who are the house-breakers, impertinent, marauding toughs without respect for property or rank. The television detective daren't be a social avenger. To enfeeble him, television makes him a ghastly but harmless monster (Kojak, Cannon and co.) or even an item of middle-class interior decor like the set itself (the angels with their limbs slinkily extended across the plush sofas of Charlie's consulting-room).

Because the living room where the set is placed becomes the theatre of values to which television programmes must adapt themselves, the medium can cope neither with the righteous logic of detection nor with radical journalism. The reports from Vietnam may have, over the years, persuaded the American voters to lose faith in the administration's policies, but for typically televisual reasons: the war was improperly intruding into their living rooms, showing them things they preferred not to see, so stopping the war was like switching off the set, disconnecting reality. Insurers in the wealthy suburbs even nominate the television set as the guardian of its fellow commodities, suggesting that owners use time-switches so it can play in their absence and warn off burglars. The only abuses television is concerned to rectify are those within its personal province of consumerism. On the channel 4 news in New York the implacable Betty Furness – former advertiser of Westinghouse fridges and Lyndon Johnson's special assistant on consumer affairs – nags into submission manufacturers or repairers who have ripped off their clients. But the BBC's equivalent of Betty Furness, Esther Rantzen, has televisually trivialised the detection of consumer frauds by presenting

them as circumlocutory entertainments. The title of her programme, *That's Life*, invites amused, defeated acceptance not
angry objection to the capitalist misdemeanours and
bureaucratic obfuscations she narrates. Whereas Betty Furness with her business suits and owlish mien resembles a fero-
cious judge, Esther Rantzen attires herself for her programme
in frilly negligees and reels off the horror stories of bam-
boozled and distraught consumers as gigglingly protracted
comic anecdotes. The criminality of petty bourgeois gangsters
and the exhausting indecisiveness of government departments
are alike material for jokes. One of her co-presenters, Cyril
Fletcher, a demobbed panto dame, wears evening dress, sits in
a leather chair, and leeringly recites smutty misprints from
provincial newspapers which viewers have sent in. The detection of faults and abuses is thus cognate, so far as *That's Life* is
concerned, with the prurient uncovery of doubles-entendres.

I have suggested that character on television is conceived as
an impediment, a humbling offence against the bland, mild,
characterless type – Cannon's *embonpoint*, Kojak's depilated
skull, Ironside's paralysis. Stardom on television is equally
invidious. The movie star compels everyone to subscribe to his
or her self-image. Stardom in the movies is a fiction of omni-
potence (Valentino as a sheik, Bette Davis as a flouncing auto-
cratic Elizabeth I) or even of sanctity (Garbo wanted to play
Francis of Assissi and commissioned Aldous Huxley to write a
treatment of his life for her). The star is one who compels
others, as Garbo did with Huxley, to believe in his or her aura,
to invent adventures for his or her rampant self-image. But the
movies also permit a freedom to experiment with the image, to
query and disown it. Hence the fad of films in which stars
played a pair of roles, confronting and controverting the image
to which they'd previously adhered. In *The Whole Town's
Talking*, Edward G. Robinson, the most placid and cultivated
of men, outfaced and dissociated himself from his own
cinematic image as a criminal degenerate. He plays both a

ravening gangster and a timid, poetically dreamy clerk who happens to be the gangster's double. After a series of confusions, the clerk exterminates the public enemy, and in doing so Robinson casts off the caricature of the image. Bette Davis achieves the same feat of self-renovating self-extinction in *A Stolen Life*, where she plays identical twins. The tender, loyal sister loses Glenn Ford to her unscrupulous, unfaithful look-alike, who is a parody of a Davis heroine. In a boating accident the wicked sister drowns, and the other, fighting to save her, pulls off her wedding ring. Thereafter she impersonates the sister who's dead, and can thus reclaim the husband her twin has purloined. The plot isn't meant as psychological realism but as a metaphor for the star's liberty to cancel (which means kill) an image which she feels traduces her. When the spurned good sister is accused of nervy frigidity by Dane Clark, Davis cries, 'But I wasn't always like this! People change!' It's the actress's own complaint, her repudiation of a false version of herself.

Television provides no such opportunities for self-contradiction. Stardom on television is experienced by its beneficiaries as a limitation and an ignominy not, as in the movies, an access of monarchical power or an ascension to the company of divinity. The television star is someone who has been made the victim of a stereotype, and who feels cramped and depreciated by its strictures. He longs to shed the image which has supererogated his own reality, and battles frantically to break out of the box. Henry Winkler, donating the Fonz's scuffed leathers to the Smithsonian and priding himself on his Yale credentials as a drama student, resents the programme to which he owes his celebrity and irritably corrects infants who yell, 'Hi Fonzie!' at him, explaining that his name is Winkler. He has even, in his desperation to disburden himself of the stereotype, appeared in a CBS special on Shakespeare. Farrah Fawcett, asked by Barbara Walters what she'd accomplished by resigning from *Charlie's Angels*, reported that she's

bursting with growth' (a Californian trope: she describes herself
as if she were vegetation) and exults that she can now 'be
herself'. But what self has she to be? In her case, the pin-up's
the reality. She's engaged in the television personality's futile
quest to acquire a third dimension.

The type may, as in the case of *Charlie's Angels*, seem
benign, but the stereotype is malignant, and its most pathetic
victims are the actors on the soap operas. They're required by
their contracts to conduct their private lives as extensions of
the fiction: morality clauses empower the producers to dismiss
a performer if he or she violates the sudsy probity which the
serials defend. Yet at the same time they're punished in their
own persons for the malfeasances of the characters they play.
The soap actors have a sorry history of bruises and buffetings,
administered by a censorious public. Margaret Mason, when
playing Linda in *Days of Our Lives*, had a carton of milk
poured over her in a supermarket by a consumer outraged at
the character's perfidy; Eileen Fulton, playing the bitchy Lisa
in *As The World Turns*, was clubbed with a handbag by
another viewer who shrieked while beating her, 'I hate you!'
Paranoia is an occupational ailment for these people. When
Rachel Ames as Audrey was flirting extra-maritally in *General
Hospital* she was accosted and abused by a man who claimed
that his wife had been so upset by her vicious goings-on that
she'd almost suffered a heart attack. When her character was
on trial for murder, Rachel Ames was convinced that shop
assistants were punishing her by refusing to wait on her. In
spite of their protests, these actors have been subsumed by
their roles. Virginia Dwyer, who plays Mary Matthews in
Another World, sums up the soap performer's paranoid alarm
when she realises that her identity has been confiscated by the
fiction: 'One afternoon I returned home from the studio and
began poking around in my clothes closet. Suddenly I reeled
from the shock. Every article of clothing in that closet was
Mary's, not mine. Every dress and every coat was exactly

her – ultraconservative. I panicked. I scooped all the clothes up in my arms and threw them out!'

Another television character who disowned the stereotype as violently as Virginia Dwyer is Donna Reed. In the 1950s she had her own show, in which she played an immaculate and emollient housewife, dispensing milk, cookies and homey wisdom to her brood. After a few seasons she became disenchanted with the homiletic idyll, at first demanding more money, then resigning from the show and reviling its suburban decencies. She divorced her husband, began campaigning against the Vietnam war, and as a newly liberated woman harangued the male television programmers who had invented the 'two-dimensional, stereotyped' Donna Stone. Others have confessed a milder distaste for the characters with which television has afflicted them. Nancy Walker on *Rhoda* played a stifling Jewish matriarch, oppressing her offspring with her love. Even in her commercials for Bounty paper towels, sucking spills into those absorbent quilts, she's a declassed Ida Morgenstern, fanatical about a clean counter. But the actress takes care to dissociate herself from her televisual identity: 'I've met her eight million times,' she says of Rhoda's mother, 'but she has no life away from her children.' Another harried spouse, Jean Stapleton as Edith Bunker from *All in the Family*, so resented the dumb role she was required to play that she began imploring the script writers to kill her. If she continued, she was sure that the caricature would consume her: 'people will never think of me as anyone else.' In 1980 the producers obliged and sentenced Edith to death. She had to expire off-camera, however: Jean Stapleton declined even to make a valedictory appearance.

Quitting the fantasy doesn't always help, because it is reality which television is slandering. Esther Rolle, the black mother in *Good Times*, departed because she objected to the insulting conception of her son on the show, the street-corner entrepreneur J.J. But she found that without her the show became even more obnoxious. The writers had additionally conspired to blame Esther Rolle by sending her character, Florida Evans, off on an indefinitely protracted honeymoon, leaving the shiftless J.J. in charge of the family. The actress objected that the character was being used against her: 'A mother just wouldn't do that,' she complained. Her maternal role had been assumed by a neighbour, the gamey Willona, who to establish her familial credentials was ordered to adopt a battered child. Esther Rolle smarted too at this turn of events. The fantasy had now become a libel on reality. Would the social services, Rolle demanded, entrust a child to a gadabout like Willona? At this stage the quarrel over the show's direction had turned into a war of opposing stereotypes, for the actress playing Willona, when offered the part, had refused to play 'a mother of three kids who loved to bake and cook', declaring that 'the days of the black mammy are over'. Instead she wanted to be a rapacious and unattached careerist. The writers at first yielded to her, but when they needed a surrogate for Esther Rolle they redomesticated her. Rolle meanwhile was disputing the right of this inimical stereotype to invade her territory. Eventually she had to capitulate. The only way of expelling the caricatures which had triumphed in her absence was to return to the show.

One at least of television's unfortunate legatees died in his despairing effort to shed the medium's stereotype. George Reeves couldn't get a job when the *Adventures of Superman* ceased production, because to those who might have hired him he had no existence except as the man from Krypton, and he committed suicide in 1959. Leonard Nimoy, one of Reeves's extra-terrestrial colleagues, wrote a book indignantly insisting *I Am Not Spock*, but in the course of it he admits that he did unwittingly turn into the hermetic spike-eared creature he plays on *Star Trek*. When the series was being planned, there was a scheme to plaster Nimoy in make-up so thickly that his identity would remain a mystery. To the credulous public, he would seem an 'actual alien', unavailable in private life. Nimoy approved this stratagem, which would camouflage him: 'I could do the job, earn the money and avoid the dangers of being connected with a ludicrous character.' But though this plan was rejected, the success of the series did make an alien of Nimoy. Mobbed whenever he showed himself in public, flinching from the inevitable question 'What happened to your ears?' just as Jean Stapleton recoiled from the jovial assaults of the fans who hailed her as 'Dingbat!' in the street, Nimoy began to crave the privacy and inscrutability enjoyed by Spock, and made sure he was accorded it. Not only had he been deprived of his own identity, he was also charged with mimicking the caricature he had invented. Once the series became a fad, Nimoy was one among a million Spocks, all with foam rubber tips over their ears. During a session of group therapy he was asked what neurosis it was which made him try so hard to look like 'that Mr Spock on television'.

The safest and most lucrative policy is to acquiesce in the caricature, as Larry Hagman has done. Interviewed on the BBC in April 1980, he sauntered on dressed as J.R., with boots, stetson and a horn-tipped stick to brandish, bridling at the complimentary hisses from the audience and admitting that he's now unable to rid himself of the serpentine Texan drawl he affected for the series. The cunning self-exploiter no longer distinguishes between the reality and the fantasy: 'did you see the episode', he asked his interviewer, 'in which I become a billionaire?' Hagman has embraced the stereotype and (learning from J.R. how to deal with the producers of the show) made it pay, literally converting it into currency by minting a series of $100 bills adorned with the leering face of J.R. which he distributes to those who pester him for autographs. It's a gesture which both enforces the stereotype and mocks it: Hagman is purchasing leisure, preferring to issue $100 bribes rather than go to the trouble of scribbling his name, and his gimmick has a profligacy worthy of the character; but there's also a calculated ironic inappropriateness to it – imagine J.R.

giving away so much money, merely in order to curry favour. At the same time, Hagman is exemplifying the likely redundancy of his own stardom, spending himself, for the images he hands out are valuable not as currency but as souvenirs, printed ephemera, the remnants of a craze which will soon be forgotten. On television, Hagman knows, only oblivion awaits him. 'It's not going to last forever,' he remarked in another interview, 'and I hope to sit out the next down period with equanimity.' Cashing in on J.R., he was subsidising the anonymity ahead, aware that television will soon indifferently efface him. When he arrived at Madame Tussaud's to confront a wax effigy of himself, he was asked by a television newsman how long he expected the cult to last. 'For the next three or four seconds,' he replied. It was an exact and a promptly self-fulfilling prophecy, for within three or four seconds the amnesiac screen had indeed expunged him.

10
Box

This essay hasn't been intended as a satire. Its aim is neither punitive nor corrective. I for one won't stop watching television. Nor, I suppose, will I stop feeling guilty about doing so. My concern has been simply to notice what happens in and on television, to watch the way its form encroaches on or determines content – and this inquiry into the relation between form and content is the fascination not of television alone but of all media and all artistic genres. Television's programmes are meditations on the medium itself. The soaps, for instance, are – like television – about how to pass time, how to keep occupied while doing nothing. Soap characters are becalmed in a crisis-ridden, urgent, panicking condition of utter stasis. Life on the soaps is a protracted and vacant afternoon – an afternoon coextensive with the one we're listlessly spending in front of the television watching the soaps. The ads and the game shows proclaim the television set's function as a commodity, dedicated to the promotion of its fellow commodities, an item of furniture which is forever enticing us to buy other items of furniture and houses to lodge the furniture in and polishes and waxes to clean the furniture with and designer jeans and cars and any other merchandise which will earn us our furniture's respect. The news too absorbs the world and fits it into the television set, where newsreaders double as newsmakers.

A multiplicity of images is diverted into the box, but, once they're inside, the medium takes control, blurring and eliding those different messages until we can no longer tell them apart. An American friend in whose house I sometimes watch television is a restless and impatient wielder of one of those devices which change channels by remote control. He's fond of flicking through the range of stations available in a quick and tetchy sequence. Used like this, the station-changer equalises those competing channels. The commercials merge: the set is a supermarket aisle, stocked with rows of warring but indistinguishable products, separable only thanks to their brand names and their packaging. Different programmes are pulped and mashed into a composite. On Easter Sunday 1980 we darted – pausing a few seconds on each channel – in rotation between a Munich performance of Bach's *St John Passion*, in which the visual distraction was the pages of a Gothic breviary narrating the stations of the cross; a documentary about a crucifixion play enacted with crude fervour by peasants in the mountains of Brazil; the mechanical miracles of de Mille's *Ten Commandments*; and the swooning baroque sensuality of Zeffirelli's *Jesus of Nazareth*. Jumping from mass to pageant, from Western epic in Biblical costume to Italian sacred opera without music, from one age and one continent to all others, we were encouraging television's indiscriminate mastication of its material and its contraction of the world to the size of the self-absorbed box. Television's plenitude is that of the supermarket: an array of spurious alternatives; innumerable competing versions of the same thing.

With people too television enforces a strict typology. Its characters are pressed out, identical as are those supermarket wares, from moulds – the corps of interchangeable game show hosts, individualised only by a gimmicky salute or a perky catch-phrase or a bad habit like Richard Dawson's kisses; Charlie's seasonally replenished sorority of angels; the jesting committees of newscasters for whom the day's events are shared repartee. This, as the previous chapter has argued, sabotages drama on television. Success means acquiescence in a type. Some legatees of this success spurn it, shedding the type and sentencing either their caricature (like Jean Stapleton) or themselves (like George Reeves) to death. But while these ingrates fret to escape from the box, others are comfortably housed there. Larry Hagman exploits the type to which he's been relegated, and sees to it that he's well reimbursed for his self-vilification. Milton Berle, condemned to appear on a show called *Jackpot Bowling* with a ration of one minute and forty-five seconds for his opening patter, adapted his act to the grudging interval of time allowed him: one minute and forty-five seconds, he calculated, 'means about nine jokes if I talk fast. I talk fast.' The great television performer – Johnny Carson, for instance – is one who doesn't resent his confinement by the medium but rejoices in it. Carson takes the rules which govern television's unreality and, as we watch, he dangerously flouts them. His interlocutors aren't guests but a succession of strangers booked by his talent co-ordinator, to whom he asks questions written out on cards for him by a researcher; the room in which these simulated conversations happen is itself a pseudo-place, flimsily erected in the corner of a studio. Carson's comedy exposes the feint and delights in it.

His sardonic reduction of the room to a set abets another of television's inclinations. The box purports to be our window on the world. But the only place to which it gives us access is the studio, a larger and more snugly insulated box. The world as conceived by television is a synoptic box. The newsrooms with their chattering teletype machines and rows of clocks keeping the time on five continents and their views of cut-out skylines present the studio as the planet's headquarters; the game shows and the ads take place in a combination of hypermarket and casino, an emporium of fantasy which could only be constructed in the studio; the sitcoms all seem to be set in the same congested but anonymous housing project. Bob

Box

Newhart felt himself to be cooped in this boxy domicile with unbearable neighbours, which is why he resigned from his own show in 1977: 'if we'd gone another year, they'd have had a guy and two girls living in the apartment above us, and a Martian living on the ground floor next door to three girl detectives. That way we'd have had all the elements of what passes for a hit sitcom this year.' Even outer space, when seen on television, resembles nothing so much as a television studio. During the moonshot, live relays from the moon alternated with studio mock-ups, and it was often difficult to tell which was which, especially as the lunar waste looked like a cheerless studio in the sky. Wits in certain quarters remain convinced that the whole enterprise was a bluff, a carnival of special effects staged in a studio somewhere to justify the $24 billion levied in taxes to subsidise the alleged exploration (which was even given the televisual title of 'the space programme', half conceding that it was only a show).

Television hopes to intern all of us in its simulatory box. Disneyworld at Orlando, Florida has already done so inside its Space Mountain: here a clown soothes a toy tot by aiming at it the electronic comforter of a television camera, while a cybernetic youth learns to ski in front of a videotaped alpine slope. Already the gadgetry of this abstract future is on sale. You can buy in cartridge form a basketball game which plugs into a computer and can be played on your television screen, sealing you off from the open air and the energetic excitement of athletic contest and transferring you to an animated simulacrum in two dimensions. The computer, unfailingly resourceful, will dribble, pass, shoot or intercept the ball, and can stand in as a player if you can't raise the requisite number. Forced to choose between life and television, the medium's loyalists will cleave to its unreality. Alan Whicker included in his 1980 series on Californian eccentricities a tour of duty with the San Francisco police. One of his outings in the squad car took him to a grubby hotel where a drug dealer had been beaten insensible by a dissatisfied customer. In the hotel lobby a group of residents was watching a detective drama on television. The police, Whicker's camera crew and the ambulance men careened through, but, unperturbed by the sirens and the confusions, none of the television-watchers, Whicker reports, deigned to look away from the screen. They might perhaps have condescended to watch the incident later on the news.

We have almost been persuaded not to accredit the reality of anything unless we can experience it at second hand, mediated by the television cameras. In one of the video magazines recently I found a plaintive letter from a couple in Pennsylvania, who were readying themselves to have a child by Caesarean section and had obtained permission to make a videotape of events in the operating room. All their anxieties, in anticipation of the surgical delivery, were technical: 'What type of colour camera should we buy or rent? Which one would give us the best angles for close-ups and best colour quality?' The magazine, in replying, perfunctorily congratulated them, but reserved its most sympathetic concern for the health of their video machinery: 'don't forget to ask hospital personnel about whether or not your equipment needs to be specially sanitized.' Theirs was to be an electronic infant, born on and into the box.